THE
NUCLEAR FREEZE MOVEMENT

JUDITH BENTLEY

A GROLIER COMPANY

FRANKLIN WATTS ■ 1984
NEW YORK ■ LONDON ■ TORONTO ■ SYDNEY

Photographs courtesy of
Wide World Photos: pp. 8, 29, 43, 82, 104, 106;
Union of Concerned Scientists: p. 62.

Library of Congress Cataloging in Publication Data

Bentley, Judith.
The nuclear freeze movement.

Bibliography; p.
Includes index.
Summary: Discusses the history of the arms race
and the growth of the nuclear freeze movement.
Explains how the freeze would work and examines
the arguments for and against it.
1. Atomic weapons and disarmament—
Juvenile literature.
2. Antinuclear movement—
Juvenile literature. I. Title.
JX1974.7.B455   1984   327.1′74   83-23449
ISBN 0-531-04772-5

CONTENTS

THE NUCLEAR FREEZE MOVEMENT

INTRODUCTION

Most books about nuclear war begin with a bang—with a description of the horror of an all-out nuclear exchange. Everyone should read one of these accounts (such as the first chapter of *Nuclear War: What's in It for You?* by the Ground Zero organization). Everyone should know what the likelihood of survival would be in the event of a nuclear war and what that survival would be like.

But this book begins, instead, with the wings of a dove on a person's outstretched hand. The dove, long a symbol of peace, and the outstretched hand, a symbol of human effort, are one of the logos of the freeze movement.

The freeze movement is a collection of diverse people who are united around an idea—a nuclear weapons freeze—as a way to prevent nuclear war. These people have heard lectures on the medical consequences of nuclear war or seen movies about the arms race and have been moved to do something about it. The slogan that accompanies the dove-in-hand logo—"The Future in Our Hands"—explains why they've decided to act.

The freeze movement has been supported by many people who are advocates of peace. Not all of them are working for a freeze, but they all in some way support a halt to the arms race.

The symbols that are meaningful to them are also diverse. One is the "ban-the-bomb boogie" which Dr. Judith Lipton, a Seattle psychiatrist and parent of three children, wears on a chain around her neck. Dr. Lipton works with a group called Physicians for Social Responsibility. The "boogie" is the 1960s peace symbol—an inverted Y with an extra spoke inside of a circle. Dr. Lipton's five-year-old daughter calls the emblem the "ban-the-bomb boogie" and says it will protect her from nuclear war.

Another symbol is a bicycle wheel with spokes arranged in the same peace symbol. The bicycle wheel is the sign of the Peace Pedallers, a group of six young adults who left California in the spring of 1982 and bicycled across the country, sharing with church and youth groups their thoughts on peace.

Still another symbol for peace is the Federation of American Scientists sticker on the cabinet door in Kitty Mattes's kitchen in Ithaca, New York. Her son put it there. Over a mushroom cloud on a red background the sticker proclaims, "Nuclear War Is National Suicide." There are many other symbols of groups and people striving for peace, including a dove over a broken bomb and a mushroom cloud with a banning sign over it.

All of these symbols, people, and groups have come together around one central idea: a nuclear weapons freeze. A nuclear weapons freeze means that the United States and the Soviet Union would agree to immediately halt the arms race. Both countries would stop testing, producing, and deploying nuclear weapons.

The official wording is a "mutual freeze on the testing, production, and deployment of nuclear weapons and of missiles and new aircraft designed primarily to deliver nuclear weapons." Both superpowers would keep the weapons, missiles, and bombers they have already produced, for the time being, but they would not add anything new. A freeze would halt the production of cruise missiles, the MX missile, the Pershing 2, the Trident II missile, new warheads, Soviet intercontinental missiles, the Backfire bomber, and intermediate-range missiles such as the SS-20. (These weapons and their capabilities will be described in a later chapter.) A freeze would be followed by negotiations for reductions in stockpiles of weapons.

The freeze is not a new idea; it was first proposed by an American arms-control negotiator in Geneva in 1964. The United States Senate actually passed a freeze resolution by a large vote in 1970. And the Russians have proposed a freeze to the United Nations every year since 1976. But the American public was not ready to consider a freeze until the early 1980s.

Randall Forsberg, an American woman who had lived in Sweden and then studied defense at MIT, became concerned about the ever-escalating arms race. After a speech she gave to peace groups in Louisville, Kentucky, she wrote a four-page suggestion for a freeze. Her "Call to Halt the Nuclear Arms Race" was published in April 1980 and gained the support of peace groups. They began working together to get it adopted, and the Nuclear Weapons Freeze Campaign was born.

The idea of a nuclear freeze caught on quickly. It was simple, immediate, and understandable to most people, unlike some of the complicated provisions of arms-control treaties. After talking to many church and college groups about the arms race Forsberg felt she should push for just one thing at a time. "So I started giving public talks that said that we should have a very modest goal of just stopping the making of any more nuclear weapons." Her simple proposal became the rallying point for the fastest growing political movement of our time. Just two years later, 75 percent of Americans polled said they favored a mutual nuclear weapons freeze.

Why does the freeze appeal to so many people? A second generation is now "growing up nuclear" under the shadow of the atomic bomb. The mushroom cloud has haunted us since the atomic bomb was dropped in 1945. American children born as atomic bombs were dropped on Japan hid under their school desks and in the halls during 1950s air raid drills. As young people and parents they became concerned about the effects of radioactive fallout and the safety of nuclear power in the 1960s and 1970s. The Vietnam War aroused skepticism over America's military commitments. Then, in the early 1980s, President Ronald Reagan talked as if a nation could fight, win, and survive a nuclear war. The children of the 1950s worried about their own children's survival.

You are the second generation to grow up in the nuclear age. Why should you read a book about the freeze? Because soon you may have a chance to vote on the issue or for candidates who advocate the freeze or another way to prevent nuclear war.

Nuclear annihilation has been called the most crucial issue of our time. Just a few of the approximately 50,000 nuclear weapons now possessed by the United States and the Soviet Union could destroy all the cities in the northern hemisphere in merely half an hour. Life as we know it would end.

Nuclear war is a subject many people have wanted to avoid. Moreover, the ordinary person feels unable to do much about the nuclear threat.

"We tend to trivialize it [nuclear war], deny its seriousness, or blot it completely out of our thinking," said psychologist Dr. Carl Rogers. "The trivialization of the horror of nuclear war is shown in the popular video games of missiles and satellites falling on cities. . . . We are making nuclear war thinkable by treating it as though it were just a game."

The recent open talk about nuclear war by public officials has alarmed many Americans out of their passivity. Dr. Helen Caldicott, a pediatrician who influenced many people to join the antinuclear movement, explained: "To know is terrifying, but not to know may be fatal."

Freeze advocates say the freeze is a strong first step away from nuclear war. Is the freeze our best hope? Will it stop the arms race? If it does, will that prevent nuclear war? This book will search for answers to those questions. Chapter 1 will look at the history of the arms race, focusing on how the second half of the twentieth century became the nuclear age and what keeps the arms race going still. After a brief look at early peace movements, Chapter 2 will show how a later peace movement developed in the late 1970s and early 1980s in Australia and Europe. The growth of the freeze movement in the United States will be described in Chapter 3. Chapter 4 will explain how a nuclear weapons freeze would work.

Important arguments for a freeze will be presented in Chapter 5. Chapter 6 will look at some drawbacks to the freeze and at its major opposing idea—peace through strength. Chapter 7 examines steps toward peace that might come after a freeze and alternatives to a freeze. Included are suggested actions anyone can take to help prevent nuclear war. Each chapter is preceded by a profile of a person who is working in some way for peace.

By the end of this book, you should know enough about the freeze to make up your mind on the issue. And once you confront the possibility of nuclear war, you will find there is something you, too, can do about it.

1

HOW DID WE GET INTO THIS MESS?

A prominent group of scientists has described the 1980s and the years ahead as a new age of instability, years when nuclear war is becoming increasingly probable. If this prediction by the Union of Concerned Scientists is true, how did we get into this mess? What forces have brought us to the brink of destruction?

The atomic bomb was created forty years ago out of fear—fear that Hitler would get the bomb first, that the Germans would have it before we did. Scientists Otto Hahn and Fritz Strassman had made a discovery in Berlin in 1938 that paved the way for the bomb. They succeeded in splitting the nucleus of a uranium atom by bombarding it with a stream of neutrons. The splitting process they discovered—fission—provided the explosive power for the atomic bomb.

Scientists who had left Germany just before World War II worried that scientists still there knew enough about fission to build a bomb for Hitler. (They were not, in fact, building one.) Albert Einstein, who had left Germany in 1933, was persuaded to write a letter to President Roosevelt urging him to build a bomb fast. Financier Alexander Sachs delivered the letter and convinced Roosevelt to start a top secret program, eventually known as the Manhattan Project. Einstein later considered the letter the worst mistake of his life.

In two years, scientists were able to set off a nuclear chain reaction under part of the football stadium at the University of Chicago. Two and a half years later the Manhattan Project produced a bomb, which was tested in New Mexico on July 16, 1945. In August President Truman decided to drop atomic bombs on two Japanese cities to encourage an end to the war in the Pacific. An atomic bomb was dropped on Hiroshima on August 6 and on Nagasaki on August 9, 1945.

The uranium bomb dropped by a single B-29 on Hiroshima had an explosive power of 15,000 tons of TNT. The plutonium bomb dropped on Nagasaki was equal to 20,000 tons of TNT. Together they killed about 150,000 people and injured thousands more, some of whom are still dying from cancer caused by the radioactive fallout. Of the 90,000 buildings in Hiroshima, 62,000 were destroyed. Sixty-five of the city's 150 doctors were dead immediately and most of the rest were severely injured. All but about 100 of the 1,780 nurses were dead or too injured to work. Japan surrendered little more than a week later.

The world was stunned. National leaders saw the bomb in political terms and recognized that a new type of warfare had been introduced.

Immediately proposals were made to stop the bomb. The United Nations had just been established when it drafted a resolution to set up an Atomic Energy Commission with the goal of eliminating atomic weapons. In June 1946 Bernard Baruch presented a plan to the United Nations from the United States to prohibit the further manufacture of nuclear weapons. Since the United States already had the bomb and the Soviets didn't, the Soviets weren't eager to freeze the status quo. The U.S.S.R. proposed destroying all existing nuclear weapons and stopping production, but the United States would not agree. So, with only three bombs built, the arms race was on.

**More than two-thirds of the city of
Hiroshima was destroyed by an atomic bomb
dropped on August 6, 1945.**

Everyone except physicists thought it would take the Russians twenty years to develop an atomic bomb, but they had one by 1949. In 1952 the United States tested a hydrogen bomb, based on the principle of fusion rather than fission. (Energy is released by the joining of nuclei of atoms, rather than the splitting of nuclei.) Great Britain tested an atomic bomb in 1953, and France had one ready by 1959.

THE ARMS RACE
GAINS MOMENTUM

At first the arms race was a contest to build bigger and better bombs. The bombs that were dropped on Hiroshima and Nagasaki each exploded with a force less than 1 megaton (which is equal to the force of one million tons of TNT). By 1961 the Soviets had exploded a 50-megaton bomb, and the superpowers turned to stockpiling bombs. By December of 1953, the United States had 3,000 to 4,000 and the U.S.S.R. had 300 to 400.

The arms race next developed delivery systems that could carry bombs farther, faster. The B-29 that dropped the bombs on Japan were propeller bombers. By 1948 the United States had an intercontinental bomber, which the Soviets did not achieve until 1955.

H-bombs, which were much smaller than A-bombs and relatively cheap, could be carried in missiles. The Soviets developed an ICBM (intercontinental ballistic missile) in 1957 and the United States had one a year later. In the 1960s and 1970s intercontinental ballistic missiles were developed that could carry a bomb 5,000 to 6,000 miles (8,000 to 9,600 km) with great accuracy. Submarines were also fitted with missiles that could be launched from the sea. Each side eventually developed three different ways to deliver bombs: bombers, missiles launched from the ground, and missiles launched from submarines. This diversity of delivery systems is called a *triad approach.*

After each power had missiles that could reach the other, they began working on antiballistic missile systems, or ABMs. The United States had developed a method of shooting down incoming missiles by 1972. ABM systems were curtailed, however, by SALT I, Strategic Arms Limitation Talks that resulted in an agreement between the United States and the Soviet Union in 1972.

Even before SALT I was signed, an ominous new technological advance was made—MIRVs. Pioneered by the United States in the late 1960s, MIRVs are multiple, independently-targetable re-entry vehicles. This means that the last stage of a missile (the re-entry vehicle that comes back into the earth's atmosphere) can have several warheads, each for a different target. One MIRVed missile, for example, can drop ten different bombs on ten different cities. The failure to ban MIRVs, during the SALT talks, is regarded by some as "the single most destabilizing decision in the arms race."

In addition to warheads and missiles, smaller battlefield weapons were devised. Battlefield nuclear weapons are less powerful and can't go as far as the standard ones. They can be fired from tanks, cannons, and grenade launchers and deployed as landmines or as underwater explosives. They are referred to as *tactical;* the long-range weapons are *strategic.* Some 14,000 tactical weapons are now stationed around the world with American and NATO troops.

While the race between the Soviet Union and the United States proceeded, other countries learned how to make bombs and bought the material to make them. Six countries now have nuclear bombs: the United States, the Soviet Union, Britain, France, China, and India. Two probably have them but won't admit it—Israel and South Africa. Four others could build them and seven more are working on it, including Pakistan, Iraq, Libya, and Egypt.

Israel bombed Iraq's nuclear reactor on June 7, 1981 to keep a hostile neighbor from having the bomb.

In just thirty-five years, the world's stockpile of nuclear weapons went from 1 to 50,000—many times more than would be needed if someone intentionally set out to destroy our planet. With as few as one hundred warheads, each of the superpowers could destroy the other. Every day three to five more hydrogen bombs are constructed.

Why did the two superpowers continue to race when enough was clearly enough? Jerome Wiesner, president emeritus of the Massachusetts Institute of Technology (M.I.T.), has described the arms race as a race with ourselves: "We'd invent a weapon, then we'd invent a defense against it, then we'd defend the next weapon because the Russians would have built what we'd invented." The Soviets tended to lag five years behind us in technology and were always struggling to catch up. (See the chart on page 19.)

The race was constantly fed by the fear that the other side had more, that a gap was developing. In the late 1940s and early 1950s there was talk of a bomber gap. At their Air Show in 1955 the Soviets displayed ten of their first long-range bombers. The same ten bombers kept flying past the reviewing stand, creating an impression of strength that was in fact very shallow. The United States overreacted. After that display the U.S. Air Force estimated the Soviet Union could produce 600 of the bombers within two years if they tried hard, which would give them a two-to-one advantage. President Eisenhower broke off arms limitation talks with the Soviet Union in 1956 because of this possible advantage. In fact the Soviet Union never produced more than 300 long-range bombers, and the United States easily held its large advantage, with 500 B-52s and more than 1,500 B-47s.

A missile gap was feared by Americans in the 1960s. A report given to President Eisenhower concluded the Russians could have enough ICBMs by 1959 to wipe out the

American bombers. Eisenhower thought much of the analysis was wrong, but the report was leaked to the press. John Kennedy used the rumor of a missile gap to help defeat Richard Nixon in the 1960 election. The rumor faded soon after that.

THE COLD WAR

The arms race was also fueled by the animosity between the Soviet Union and the United States. Had the two countries been friendly after World War II, the arms race might never have begun. But mutual suspicion and distrust set in right after the war. Having suffered the loss of twenty million people, the Soviet Union said it needed Eastern European nations as a buffer against future invasions. The United States had little sympathy for the territory grab.

The cold war that followed was a war fought with words backed up by the threat of using the bomb. The dropping of the atomic bomb on Japan was less the end of World War II, it has been said, than the first act of the cold war with Russia, to show them what we could do. Once the Russians had the bomb, too, the superpowers raced to keep their threats credible. Premier Khrushchev went so far as to promise, "We will bury you."

Secretary of State John Foster Dulles, who served under President Eisenhower, also made the threat explicit. In a famous speech in 1954 he spoke of "massive retaliation." He said the United States might choose to respond to all aggression, regardless of its magnitude, with nuclear weapons.

Just by making the threat, the United States hoped to deter such aggression, without having to use force. Eisenhower thought the nation could not afford to have both a large nuclear capability and a large conventional force (the usual troops, guns, and tanks). He chose nuclear weapons because they are cheaper for the amount of harm they can do. They give "more bang for the buck."

The idea of massive retaliation was accompanied by a policy of containment, as the Soviet Union and the United States competed for influence in the world. The United States said it would act as the world's policeman and contain any Soviet aggression beyond the boundaries set after World War II. The United States tried to act on that policy until the Vietnam War showed how difficult this was to carry out.

Gradually, as the Soviet Union began to challenge America's nuclear monopoly, the policy of massive retaliation gave way to "mutual assured destruction," known simply as MAD. Both superpowers recognized that each could surely destroy the other, so it would be in neither's interest to start a nuclear war. An uneasy truce came into being.

Cold war and containment were replaced by *detente*—President Nixon and Secretary of State Henry Kissinger's policy of easing the hostility between the United States and the Soviet Union. Detente replaced confrontation with negotiation and competitive coexistence. The SALT I agreement signed in 1972 was a result of this period. The pact limited the numbers of certain weapons each country would maintain. But negotiations by the two nations on broader arms limitations were still needed. SALT II talks began.

As relations between the two countries relaxed, President Carter campaigned on the theme of controlling and reducing nuclear weapons and cutting defense spending and the export of weapons. Once in office, he felt pressures from within the country and from without that forced him to change his stance. A team of defense analysts had been asked by President Gerald Ford to second-guess the CIA's estimate of Soviet military power. Team B, as it was called, reported right after the 1976 election of Carter that the Soviet Union intended to achieve military superiority over the United States and was rapidly approaching that goal. The report claimed the Soviet Union was outspending the United States by 50 percent. Partly as a result of this report, the defense budget was raised every year Carter was in office.

Outside the country, Russian actions in the world contradicted the spirit of detente. The Soviet Union used Cuban troops to intervene in the civil war in Angola and then invaded Afghanistan in 1981. United States involvement in Vietnam also strained the spirit of detente. Coexistence seemed to mean that the superpowers would refrain from directly confronting each other, but would be free to intervene elsewhere.

When American hostages were seized in Iran in November 1979, a feeling of powerlessness was added to disillusionment with detente. All the nuclear bombs in our stockpiles were not helping solve these disputes. In response to the Iranian crisis and other events, presidential candidate Reagan criticized President Carter for pursuing a "strategy of weakness." He promised a "strategy of strength." When elected, Reagan abandoned any notion of detente and returned to cold war ideas. He saw the Russians as out to dominate the world unless the United States countered with superior military power.

President Reagan clearly disagreed that the weapons already produced were enough. At the same time Reagan initiated his strategy of strength, American nuclear policy was shifting to include the idea of nuclear warfighting. The policy of deterrence was replaced by talk of nuclear warfighting. Such warfighting would involve a limited use of nuclear weapons, limited enough to avoid all-out nuclear war.

There was also a shift in the type of weapons being developed. The new weapons were so accurate they could be used in a first strike to knock out the enemy's military bases, rather than just to retaliate. President Carter signed a directive to the military allowing them to plan nuclear attacks on the enemy's military bases.

Thus, presidents and policy shifted with international events, but the arms race never slowed down, no matter who was in office.

PEACE EFFORTS

In the thirty-five year history of the arms race, there were those who tried to stop it. Some of the first were scientists who were alarmed at what they had produced. Robert Oppenheimer, the physicist in charge of the atom bomb's development, recognized the enormity of what he had put together. As the atomic bomb was tested in July 1945, he thought of a passage from Hindu scripture: "I am become death, shatterer of worlds."

Four years later he was chairman of an advisory committee that counseled President Truman against producing the hydrogen bomb. "We believe a super bomb should never be produced . . . ," the committee reported, because it would be a weapon of mass civilian destruction, of no real military significance.

"The fact that no limits exist to the destructiveness of this weapon makes its very existence and the knowledge of its construction a danger to humanity as a whole," some committee members added. "It is necessarily an evil thing considered in any light." Despite this warning, the hydrogen bomb was built and gradually replaced the atomic bomb in the U.S. arsenal.

Two months after the bombs were dropped on Japan, dozens of nuclear physicists formed a lobbying organization called the Federation of Atomic (later American) Scientists. They succeeded in placing control of the development of atomic energy in civilian rather than military hands, but they did not achieve international control of the manufacture of atomic bombs.

Albert Einstein also opposed nuclear weapons and hoped that an informed public would act on the danger.

"To the village square we must carry the facts of atomic energy," he said in 1946. "From there must come America's voice." America was slow in finding its voice.

The first major public involvement came in response to the radiation produced by the testing of bombs in the atmosphere. On March 1, 1954, the United States exploded an H-bomb on Bikini Island in the Pacific Ocean. An unexpected change of winds swept the radiation from the blast over the inhabited Marshall Islands. It rained on a Japanese fishing vessel outside the supposed "danger zone." All of the crewmen on the boat were very ill with radiation poisoning by the time they reached port, and one crewman died six months later.

The unease created by that explosion was not erased when a reporter asked a government official how big H-bombs could be made. "Big enough to destroy any city on the face of the earth," he replied.

Prominent scientists like Einstein and Albert Schweitzer and philosopher Bertrand Russell petitioned the United Nations to call for an end to such tests. Presidential candidate Adlai Stevenson proposed during the 1956 campaign that the United States and the Soviet Union both ban testing of nuclear weapons in the atmosphere. Opponents said this was impractical because the Soviets would cheat.

Out of these concerns, a Ban-the-Bomb movement took shape in the 1950s and 1960s. New peace groups sprang up. SANE—A Citizen's Organization for a SANE World—ran an ad in *The New York Times* in 1957, calling for an end to nuclear development and testing on both sides. Within a year, more than 24,000 people had joined the cause. Bertrand Russell started the Campaign for Nuclear Disarmament (CND), which became the world's largest group for unilateral (one-sided) disarmament.

These efforts eventually paid off. In 1963, a Partial Test-Ban Treaty was signed by the United States and the Soviet Union. The treaty banned testing in the atmosphere, underwater, or in outer space.

The 1970s brought some renewed protest at the growing use of nuclear power. When President Eisenhower had attempted to soothe the public's worries in his "Atoms for Peace" speech in 1953, he emphasized the peaceful uses of atomic power and thus encouraged the development and export of nuclear power. But when other countries bought the know-how and the means to build nuclear power plants, they also bought the capability to produce plutonium and then build bombs.

Thus, by 1980 the arms race had far outrun human efforts to curb it. There were several reasons why the arms race continued:

(1) The belief that nuclear superiority gives political advantage. When the United States developed a new weapon, the Soviet Union hustled to develop the same weapon, fearing nuclear inferiority would leave it open to domination. This action-counter-action principle kept the race going.

(2) The hostility between the two superpowers. Neither country trusts the other to use restraint in world affairs or in conflicts between the two.

(3) The momentum of technology. Even as arms control agreements are made, technology outpaces the talks. One weapon might be curtailed by a treaty, but during the long negotiating process new weapons are developed.

(4) Public support for arms control was never sustained and widespread. The American public did not seem to feel directly threatened by the arms race.

So the stockpiling of weapons and modernization of delivery systems continues. Ever since 1945, a magazine called *The Bulletin of the Atomic Scientists* has featured a doomsday clock on its cover. Over the years the hands on the clock have changed position, moving closer to midnight—doomsday—as scientists calculate the probability of a nuclear war. In 1983 the hands on the clock stood at four minutes to midnight.

TIMELINE—HISTORY OF THE ARMS RACE

1939   Albert Einstein writes to President Franklin D. Roosevelt urging him to build an atomic bomb.

1943   A nuclear chain reaction is achieved under part of the football stadium at the University of Chicago. The Manhattan Project begins.

1945   A bomb is tested in New Mexico.
Atomic bomb dropped on Hiroshima.
Atomic bomb dropped on Nagasaki.

1949   Soviet Union tests its first atomic bomb.

1952   United States successfully tests a hydrogen bomb.
Great Britain explodes its first atomic bomb.

1955   Soviet Union explodes an H-bomb and displays long-range bombers.

1957   Soviet Union test flight of ICBM.
SANE is formed.

1958   United States test flight of ICBM.
Moratorium on testing in the atmosphere.

1960   France explodes its first atomic bomb.
United States deploys SLBMs.

1961   Russians explode 50-megaton bomb.

1963   Partial Test Ban Treaty (ban on testing in the atmosphere).

1964   China has the bomb.

1967   Outer Space Treaty.

1968   Non-Proliferation Treaty.

1970   United States begins deploying MIRVs.

1972   SALT I agreements, ABM Treaty.

1974   India explodes nuclear device.

1975   Soviet Union begins deploying MIRVs.

ARMS RACE DEVELOPMENTS

DEVELOPMENT	WHO INITIATED	WHEN	REACTION	WHEN
Atomic bomb	U.S.	1945	U.S.S.R.	1949
Intercontinental bomber	U.S.	1948	U.S.S.R.	1955
Hydrogen bomb	U.S.	1952	U.S.S.R.	1955
ICBM	U.S.S.R.	1957	U.S.	1958
Supersonic bomber	U.S.	1960	U.S.S.R.	1975
Submarine-launched ballistic missile	U.S.	1960	U.S.S.R.	1968
Multiple re-entry vehicles (MRVs)	U.S.	1964	U.S.S.R.	1968
ABM system	U.S.S.R.	1968	U.S.	1972
MIRVs	U.S.	1970	U.S.S.R.	1975
Neutron bombs	U.S.	1981	U.S.S.R.	none yet
Long-range cruise missiles	U.S.	198?	U.S.S.R.	none yet

Source: Copyright © 1982 by David P. Barash and Judith Eve Lipton. Reprinted by permission of Grove Press, Inc.

DR. JUDITH LIPTON

Judith Lipton is a psychiatrist in the Seattle area who devotes half of her working time to preventing nuclear war. Lipton, who is soft-spoken and barely over five feet tall, remembers when she was pregnant with her second child in Palo Alto, California. She went to lunch one day at one of the world's most prestigious think tanks at Stanford and asked about twenty people there what they thought about the possibility of nuclear war.

"To a person they said they thought nuclear war was inevitable but why should I be worrying about that on such a pretty day?" she recalled. They communicated a sense of fatalism, an attitude that there was nothing anyone could do. But the experience changed Lipton. "You don't just tell a pregnant woman that her baby's going to die in a nuclear war."

During her childhood she had been quite aware of "the bomb." Her parents, who were also physicians, knew scientists who had worked on the Manhattan Project (to develop the atom bomb) and they had participated in the Ban-the-Bomb movement of the 1950s. She remembers being told not to eat the snow in Chicago because it contained strontium 90 and could cause cancer.

The Chicago White Sox won the pennant in 1958 for the first time since 1919 and someone turned on the air raid sirens to celebrate. Everyone who wasn't watching TV thought there was a nuclear war. "I remember very clearly hearing the air raid sirens . . . wondering . . . when it was going to happen, being paralyzed with fright, looking out the window, waiting for the flash."

When her family moved to North Carolina, their house was the only one in the neighborhood without a fallout shelter. Judith resolved that in the event of a nuclear attack she would go into the bathroom, because it had no windows, and take a copy of *Gone with the Wind,* because it was the only book long enough.

Lipton did not become fully committed to trying to prevent nuclear war until a visit by Dr. Helen Caldicott to Seattle in 1980. Caldicott, a pediatrician at Boston's Children's Hospital, also traveled around the country, lecturing on the medical consequences of nuclear war.

"I spent six days chauffering her around to fifteen lectures and nine or ten radio and television interviews and heard her describe, as only Helen Caldicott can, over and over and over and over again, the medical consequences of nuclear war, and by the time she left I was"—she paused— "changed."

"Helen said, 'You have to take the world on your shoulders like Atlas. If you love this planet, you have to work to prevent nuclear war.' And I did."

What Dr. Lipton did was to leave a research job at the University of Washington and go into private practice, which gave her time to work on what Caldicott calls "political medicine." A year before, Lipton had founded the Washington chapter of Physicians for Social Responsibility (PSR). Since Caldicott's visit she has devoted two and a half years to working with PSR, lecturing, organizing educational programs, and lobbying for a stop to the arms race. She has spent a lot of time giving talks and writing, including a book she co-authored with her husband.

Speaking out against nuclear war has given her a sense of an integrated self. "I have a deep commitment to working to prevent nuclear war."

Although she remains pessimistic about the chances of preventing a nuclear holocaust, Lipton said she is much happier now that she is trying to do something about it. "Saying 'My God, we love this planet and we want to live' is the way to go."

Many other Americans, like Lipton, were ready to act on their concern in the early 1980s.

2

"IF YOU LOVE THIS PLANET"

As people became more aware of the threat of nuclear war an international peace movement was born. When the movement spread to the United States in the early 1980s it focused around the freeze. But the origins of the freeze movement were broad, building on the groundwork that was laid at home and abroad in the late 1970s.

Peace groups have always existed. Some, like the American Friends Service Committee and the Women's International League for Peace and Freedom (WILPF), have long been advocates of peace rather than war, even during World War II. Others were formed in response to the nuclear age or to recent wars. The Council for a Livable World was founded in 1962 by a nuclear physicist to warn the public and Congress of the threat of nuclear war. Clergy and Laity Concerned about the War in Vietnam protested that war in the 1960s and then became Clergy and Laity Concerned (CALC) in response to the nuclear threat. The Union of Concerned Scientists opposed nuclear power in the 1970s and then turned their attention to nuclear weapons in the 1980s.

In addition to national and international organizations, groups formed in local communities, particularly around military bases. In Poulsbo, Washington, near the West Coast Trident submarine base, a group called the Ground Zero Center for Nonviolent Action formed. Along with Live Without Trident, whose purpose is obvious from its name, they sponsored a demonstration in 1978 that drew more than four thousand people to the submarine base.

The many groups working alone were not a mass movement, however, and they had not won wide support from the general public. "The potential victims have not been brought into the debate yet," said former Defense Secretary Robert McNamara, "and it's about time we brought them in. I mean the average person." It took prodding from abroad and a series of political events to bring the average person into the debate.

Helen Caldicott, an Australian pediatrician, helped pave the way. When she was fourteen years old, Caldicott read Nevil Shute's *On the Beach*, a novel about the last survivors of a nuclear war. "I have grown up with the fear of imminent annihilation by nuclear holocaust," she said. "I am a child of the Atomic Age."

In her pediatric practice, Caldicott became alarmed when she saw children dying of cystic fibrosis, leukemia, and cancer. "I realized that these diseases would increase as the radiation in the environment increased," she wrote in her book *Nuclear Madness*. During the years she practiced medicine and had three children, France was testing nuclear bombs in the South Pacific.

Caldicott was alarmed by the tests and wrote a letter to her local newspaper. Because she was a doctor, the media paid attention to what she was saying. After that, each time France tested a bomb, she was asked to appear on television to explain the dangers of radiation. The public interest generated by those talks gained momentum when she exposed a secret government report, which said that in 1971 a high level of radiation had been found in South Australian drinking water.

The Australians were furious with the French, who admitted they never tested bombs in the Mediterranean, closer to home. "Mon Dieu, there are too many people there!" one official explained. Thousands of Australians joined marches to protest. By 1972, 75 percent of the Australian public was opposed to the tests. The Australian and New Zealand governments complained to the International Court of Justice in The Hague and finally France backed down and announced it would conduct its tests underground.

Caldicott's concern had grown into an immensely successful campaign. "One voice was all it took to raise a warning call . . . ," she wrote. "Once enough other voices joined in, that call would be heard around the world."

Three political events aroused the American and European publics. One was the failure of the United States Senate to ratify SALT II in 1979. Another was the NATO decision that same year to deploy American missiles in Europe. The third was the 1980 election of Ronald Reagan.

The slow death of the SALT II accords in the Senate marked the low point of public support for arms control. The treaty was opposed by those who thought it would give the Soviet Union an advantage. Supporters could not gain the votes of two-thirds of the Senate. The treaty was complicated and difficult for the average person to understand. When Russia invaded Afghanistan, President Carter gave up trying to win ratification. There was no sense of urgency about arms control.

President Reagan, who had campaigned on the theme of making America strong again, moved quickly to increase defense spending when he took office. One of his early decisions was to go ahead with the production of the neutron bomb, a bomb that kills people but doesn't destroy most structures. The bomb was to be used against tank forces to kill the tank crews.

Besides undertaking a military buildup, Reagan talked tough. The President told a group of newspaper editors it was possible to have a limited nuclear exchange in

Europe that would not escalate into an all-out nuclear war between the superpowers. The U.S. Secretary of Defense, Caspar Weinberger, told the military services to prepare for fighting both "limited" and "protracted" nuclear wars, implying that both are possible. Secretary of State Alexander Haig revealed that NATO has a plan to fire a nuclear warning shot if the Russians seem about to invade Europe.

Though intended to intimidate the Russians, the tough statements also alarmed Americans and particularly Europeans. Suddenly the possibility of nuclear war was being discussed by national leaders.

Explaining how this talk aroused a new peace movement, Jerome Wiesner, former president of M.I.T., said, "There has been for a long time deep-seated fear of nuclear war, but only since those in power have begun to talk openly about the prospects of fighting and winning a nuclear war have people recognized the danger. . . . In a sense this Administration has been more honest with us than its predecessors."

The Reagan administration's statements prompted activism in Europe first. Europeans were alarmed by the NATO plan to put 108 Pershing 2 missiles and 464 cruise missiles in Europe. The Carter Administration suggested equipping NATO with the missiles in 1979 to counter new Soviet intermediate-range missiles (SS-20s) deployed along the borders. The request was part of a two-track decision. The other track was to pursue arms control agreements with the Russians to limit the missiles. By 1981 plans for the missile deployment were proceeding, but arms control talks were not.

American leaders' talk of "limited" war implied to the Europeans that a nuclear war would be limited to Europe. Scottish labor leader Alex Kitson commented, "When they talk about limited nuclear war in the States, they mean it would be limited to us." Moreover, the decision to launch any of the 572 missiles in Europe would be made by the United States alone. Europe could be sacrificed without even having the power to veto such a move.

Younger Europeans found the nuclear threat more frightening than the Russian threat. They had not experienced the years of cold war distrust of the Russians as had their elders. Within a month of the December 1979 NATO decision, a new peace movement formed in Great Britain and Europe, called the Campaign for European Nuclear Disarmament (END).

END's objective is to free all of Europe from nuclear weapons, from Poland to Portugal. "We ask the two superpowers to withdraw all nuclear weapons from European territory," said an Appeal circulated in the spring of 1980. The Appeal called on the people of each nation to agitate for the expulsion of nuclear weapons and bases from European soil and territorial waters. END wants to enforce detente and take Europe out of the United States–Soviet Union confrontation.

The response to the NATO decision, to END's appeal, and to the threatening escalation of the arms race was immediate. Crowds of 70,000 to 100,000 people marched in Hamburg (West Germany), Amsterdam (the Netherlands), and Trafalgar Square (London, England) in 1980. When President Reagan took office in 1981, the numbers of demonstrators increased threefold. In the fall, crowds of 200,000 to 350,000 marched in the cities of Bonn, Rome, London, and Amsterdam.

The peace campaigns were somewhat different in each country. They were most successful in the Netherlands and Belgium. Norway, Denmark, and Sweden were already opposed to nuclear weapons on their soil. Nuclear weapons issues are hotly debated in Great Britain and West Germany. Italy's peace campaign started slowly but did achieve large demonstrations. France, with its own nuclear force, does not belong to NATO's military structure and has not been as involved in the missile deployment controversy.

The peace drive in the Netherlands became a model for other countries. It had begun before the NATO decision, in 1977. Led by the Dutch Interchurch Peace Council, the drive coalesced around the slogan, "Get rid of nuclear weapons. Let it start in the Netherlands." A crowd of 350,000 demonstrated for peace in December 1981. The crowd included military people, some high-ranking and on active duty. Largely because of the campaign, it is unlikely that the Netherlands will ever accept the forty-eight cruise missiles that NATO planned to put there.

The peace movement in Germany includes 2,000 different groups, some environmentalists, churches, and political factions. An antinuclear Green Party won twenty-seven seats in the parliament in March 1983. The main governing parties, however, continue to favor the deployment of U.S. missiles. As the date for deployment nears (late 1983), protests are expected to grow at the military bases. Germany is regarded as the front line in a Soviet invasion; 108 Pershing 2 missile launchers are to be deployed there.

In Great Britain, nuclear weapons and strategy is the second most important political issue, after the economy. The peace movement is supported by the Labour Party and the Church of England and has convinced the majority of Britons to oppose the deployment of cruise missiles there. The governing Tory Party favors the deployment of the cruise missiles and the purchase of Trident missiles from the United States.

Peace movements surfaced in other countries, too. Australians marched to oppose the mining and selling of uranium. Ten thousand Japanese demonstrators "greeted" the arrival of the U.S. aircraft carrier *Enterprise* in their port at Sasebo in 1983. The demonstrators claimed the ship may be armed with nuclear weapons, which violates Japan's "non-nuclear principles." These principles prohibit the introduction, manufacture, or storage of nuclear arms in Japanese territory.

Russia, too, has a peace movement sanctioned by the government. Soviet visitors to the United States described a "peace train" sponsored by railroad workers.

The train traveled from one end of the country to the other, collecting twenty million signatures on an appeal to the United Nations. The appeal asked the U.N. to take a more active role in arms negotiations between the superpowers.

In addition to the official movement, there is a very small unauthorized peace group in the Soviet Union which has been harassed by the government.

This international peace awakening in most cases preceded the American peace movement. "The rest of the world is more awake than America because they *know* what war is . . . ," Caldicott stated. "Modern America has never suffered war on its own soil." Caldicott called America "a sleeping giant . . . totally unaware of the incredible power it holds and the magnitude of destruction inherent in its arsenals."

The pacivity and fatalism of the American public finally gave way in the early 1980s. When Caldicott came to Boston's Children's Hospital to treat and study cystic fibrosis, she revitalized a doctors' group that had been active in the early 1960s—Physicians for Social Responsibility. Her involvement with PSR grew out of her belief that nuclear war is "the most ominous threat to public health imaginable."

PSR and the Council for a Livable World began educating the American public about the consequences of a nuclear war. PSR had been organized against nuclear power but in 1979 had dwindled to only a few members, mainly in Boston. Within a year of the date Caldicott became its president, PSR membership had grown to 12,000. In 1983 it had 30,000 members, with 180 chapters.

Caldicott crisscrossed the country giving lectures that simply described the medical consequences of nuclear war. Doctors were particularly effective at telling the story. The public had come to expect medical miracles; the doctors told them there would be no miracles after a nuclear war. Doctors and nurses themselves would be among the first casualties because they often work in

**Dr. Helen Caldicott speaks at a Mother's Day
rally for nuclear disarmament in Boston.**

urban hospitals. PSR estimated that within forty days of a major nuclear exchange, 90 percent of Americans would be dead in "the final epidemic." Since there could be no effective postwar treatment, physicians recommended prevention.

Sharing the task of educating the public were scientists, who had raised the alarm when the atomic bomb was built. Many of the leaders of the Union of Concerned Scientists were scientists at Harvard and M.I.T. Some were physicists who had worked on part of the Manhattan Project. Physicists described to audiences how bombs work and what they do. They emphasized that no one could predict the effects of a nuclear exchange because it had never been fully experienced and could not be tested.

UCS began a series of convocations on the threat of nuclear war on Veterans Day, November 11, 1981, at 155 colleges. A year later more than five hundred colleges had such convocations on the second year's theme, "solutions to the arms race." The convocations were also planned by United Campuses to Prevent Nuclear War and by PSR at medical schools and LANAC (Lawyers Alliance for Nuclear Arms Control) at law schools. Military experts and retired admirals and generals talked about the probability of nuclear war and the characteristics of the weapons at the convocations. Negotiators presented the prospects for arms control.

As a result of these educational programs, large numbers of people became alerted to the dangers of nuclear war and were willing to face the subject. Helen Caldicott had shown what a public campaign could do in Australia. Europeans had been mobilized by the prospect of large numbers of missiles on their soil. Groups like PSR and UCS had begun educating the American public, and the election of Ronald Reagan focused the choice more clearly between a military buildup and arms control. The time was right for a positive plan of action. The freeze became that plan.

Kitty Campbell Mattes was inspired to do something about the arms race in 1980, the year SALT II ratification was finally dropped and President Carter announced the resumption of registration of 18-year-olds for the draft. As a mother and stepmother of four teenagers, Mattes realized, "They're going to dress my son up in a uniform and teach him how to kill people." She felt she had to shout to the world that the arms race was wrong.

"I had been active in protests against the Vietnam War, and then I did nothing for ten years," she admitted. "I was asleep politically, like a lot of people were." But when the arms race began to affect the next generation, she decided to do something.

Since she is a writer and editor, she chose to write a book. She left a full-time job for a part-time afternoon job, which left her mornings free for research and writing. From the dining-room table of her big, old frame house in Ithaca, New York, she wrote *In Your Hands,* a compact guide to the arms race for the lay person new to the subject. A local artist designed the cover, and the book was printed locally. Mattes sold about 3,500 copies by mail from her home.

"At the time I felt very much alone," she recalled. "People patted me on the back, said what a fine thing I was doing, but they really thought it was kind of odd. But when the book came out a year later, suddenly there was a freeze movement and the timing was right."

Although she had planned to start a new organization called Parents for Peace, Mattes joined the growing freeze movement instead. She has spoken to Rotarians and local groups about the need for a freeze because "it's important that we not just talk to each other, but to the average person with five mouths to feed about the folly of spending billions of dollars on nuclear weapons." She has begun to learn about biology and how radioactivity works. She has participated in such Ithaca freeze activities as a peace rally in front of the post office on Easter morning.

In doing so she felt the support of a community and a feeling of empowerment. The cover of her book, which shows two hands cupping a village, portrays her belief in thinking positively. "The future is in our hands; we have the power to change it. We're not rebels—we're the roots. This is democracy, the people becoming aroused."

3

THE FREEZE MOVEMENT CONGEALS

U.S. citizens who had never bothered to vote stood in front of supermarkets asking their neighbors to sign nuclear freeze petitions.

"I'm not a pacifist by any means," said a former Marine Corps officer who had just participated in his first antiwar demonstration, "but when you've got enough bombs sitting around to incinerate the world ten times over, something's crazy."

A freeze had been suggested before by national leaders and discussed by several peace groups, including the American Friends Service Committee and Sojourners, an evangelical Christian ministry. President Lyndon Johnson and his Secretary of Defense, Robert McNamara, proposed "a verified freeze" through negotiators in Geneva in 1964. At that time the U.S. had a five-to-one lead in nuclear bombs, and the Soviets rejected a freeze.

A freeze resolution actually passed the Senate by a vote of seventy-three to six in 1970 at a time when the United States still had a clear advantage in nuclear arms. The proposal to halt the arms race was then called SWWA, "Stop Where We Are," but it remained just an idea. The Soviets made freeze-type proposals to the United Nations from 1976 to 1980. Republican Senator Mark

Hatfield of Oregon tried to attach a freeze as an amendment to SALT II when the Senate considered the arms control treaty for ratification in 1979, but both the amendment and the treaty never came to a vote in the Senate and so failed, in part for lack of public support.

Later that year a freeze was proposed again, and this time people listened. The person credited with popularizing the freeze idea is Randall Forsberg, a thirty-eight-year-old Barnard College English major turned defense analyst. Forsberg had worked as an editor at the Stockholm International Peace Research Institute in Sweden. When she returned to the United States, she studied political science at M.I.T., then took a leave of absence to become a full-time activist. With colleagues, she started the Institute for Defense and Disarmament Studies in Brookline, Massachusetts.

Forsberg had written a 100-page disarmament paper in 1979 which mentioned stopping the production of nuclear weapons as a first step toward disarmament. As she went around to colleges, giving speeches about the arms race, she became convinced that she should push for just one idea—the "modest" goal of stopping the production of any more nuclear weapons. SALT II had been too complex for people to understand and rally around, but a complete halt would be easy to communicate and to build support for.

"The arms race has to stop sometime, somehow," Forsberg insisted, "and it seemed to me in 1979 that we had as good a shot in the early 1980s as we ever would, if everyone focused on the same thing."

She proposed the freeze in a speech to Mobilization for Survival, a coalition of antinuclear groups meeting in Louisville, Kentucky, in December 1979. Leaders of the peace groups who heard it asked her to write up the proposal. The four-page "Call to Halt the Nuclear Arms Race," published in April 1980, became the founding document of the freeze movement.

The freeze idea was quickly adopted by peace groups.

Thirty national organizations endorsed it that summer. An umbrella organization, the National Nuclear Weapons Freeze Campaign, was formed in March 1981. Its first goal was to develop a broad and visible base of public support. Grass-roots participation grew quickly.

While the freeze idea was spreading, new peace groups were springing up overnight, each appealing to different people. LANAC (Lawyers Alliance for Nuclear Arms Control) formed early in 1981, alerted lawyers and law students to the issue. High Technology Professionals for Peace was started in March 1981 to help engineers and computer professionals find jobs unrelated to arms work. United Campuses to Prevent Nuclear War sponsored many forums and convocations on college campuses, and Educators for Social Responsibility began planning curriculums for teaching peace. Cartoonists, nurses, performing artists, students, scientists, historians, women, and others formed antinuclear groups.

Taking its name from the point on the earth directly below the center of a nuclear explosion, Ground Zero was formed in 1981 by physicist Roger Molander, a former member of the National Security Council staff. Ground Zero, which is nonpartisan, soon had chapters in 140 cities. In April 1982, during Ground Zero Week, the organization sought to educate the public about atomic destruction. More than six hundred communities and 350 college campuses participated.

Existing organizations experienced a reawakening. SANE's membership grew 80 percent in 1981. Other groups discovered the nuclear issue for the first time. The American Medical Association (AMA), a group known for its conservatism, passed a resolution urging physicians to educate themselves and their patients about the medical consequences of a nuclear attack.

The freeze campaign sought endorsements from existing groups. Eventually the freeze was endorsed by 19 labor unions, 150 national and international organizations, and by most major religious denominations.

CHURCHES AND THE FREEZE

The freeze campaign coincided with and was nurtured by the educational efforts of groups like Physicians for Social Responsibility and the Union of Concerned Scientists. It was also fed by a widespread discussion in American churches and synagogues of the moral aspects of nuclear weapons. The concern of professionals like physicians, scientists, educators, and lawyers was matched by religious leaders.

Churches have often been conservative and patriotic supporters of defense spending and of wars fought in the name of national honor. But they have come to see the possibility of nuclear war as a worldwide moral issue, a spiritual as well as an economic and political problem.

Some religious groups, like the Quakers, the Mennonites, and the Church of the Brethren, have traditionally been "peace churches." Many of their members have been pacifists, refusing to fight in wars. The majority of Christians have not been pacifists; the church has followed the "just war" theory of Aquinas. According to this theory, a war is "just" if the conflict produces more good than evil and if large populations are protected from indiscriminate injury.

The possibility of nuclear war led to a view called "nuclear pacifism"—the belief that any nuclear war is immoral, so pacifism is the only moral response.

"Southern Baptists . . . are not pacifists," explained Foy Valentine, director of the Christian Life Committee of the Southern Baptist Convention. "We support a responsible defense program, we involve ourselves in the political process, and we serve in the military forces. . . . The prospect of nuclear war, however, has ushered humanity into a new era where the killing of hundreds of millions of innocents could never be morally justified. Nuclear war can never be just war."

"It could never be morally justified to use strategic nuclear weapons," even under the "just war" theory, agreed San Francisco Archbishop John Quinn. "Any weapon that can bring about irreversible ecological damage to large portions of the earth, untold genetic damage for countless generations to come, and that can destroy in the most horrifying manner massive noncombatant populations is a colossal evil and totally immoral."

The mere threat of such a war should spur Christians to action, many religious leaders believed. "God would not be pleased if we return his creation to him in ashes," said a pastor in Lyme, Connecticut.

Lutheran, Calvinist, and Roman Catholic clergy were early organizers of the European antinuclear movement. In the United States, church leaders were also out in front on the issue. Religiously based peace groups existed prior to the freeze movement, including Pax Christi, a Catholic group; Sojourners, an evangelical Christian group; the Fellowship of Reconciliation; and Clergy and Laity Concerned. Real grass-roots participation came about when many local churches developed their own peace committees or action groups in the 1980s.

Support was so widespread, the mainline denominations began calling for a stop to the arms race. The freeze has been endorsed by the Baptists, Lutherans, Disciples of Christ, Episcopalians, Presbyterians, Unitarians, the Reformed Church, American Hebrew Congregations, the United Church of Christ, the United Methodists, and Billy Graham, among others.

Protestant theologian Harvey Cox said of the freeze, "It is not the Kingdom of God, but it may just avert the Apocalypse."

Nuclear issues were brought to the attention of Catholics during the bishops' two-year consideration of a pastoral letter. The National Conference of Catholic Bishops' Committee on War and Peace, often regarded as quite anti-Communist, began discussing a stand on the subject in 1980. They wrote and discussed three versions of a pastoral letter before a final form was ratified in May 1983.

The resulting letter urges Catholics to pay the utmost attention to achieving peace and the abolition of nuclear weapons. "We are the first generation since Genesis with the power to virtually destroy God's creation," it reads. "We cannot remain silent in the face of such danger."

The letter endorses a halt to the nuclear arms race, despite the objections of Reagan Administration officials who preferred the word "curb." Among the major statements in the letter are:

(1) Nuclear war is immoral. There can never be any justification for using nuclear weapons first.

(2) The United States should not unilaterally disarm but should take a first step toward disarmament in the expectation that the Soviet Union would reciprocate.

(3) The United States and the U.S.S.R. should renounce any intention to use nuclear weapons against civilian populations.

(4) Nuclear deterrence is justified only if accompanied by serious efforts toward disarmament.

(5) The use of nuclear bombs in a limited, less than all-out nuclear war probably isn't possible.

The 150-page letter will reach the more than five million American Catholics when it is used as a teaching resource in the consideration of war and peace issues.

Religious and moral responses to the arms race often coincide with the goals of the freeze movement, although most churches take a broader approach to peace. Not all churches, moreover, support the freeze. Evangelical television ministers who had been staunchly opposed to SALT II also oppose the freeze. Conservative evangelist Jerry Falwell says "disarmament is suicide"; others see the Russians as "a global menace." The freeze gained the support of the majority of American Christians and Jews, nonetheless.

The educational efforts of professional groups like PSR and UCS, hundreds of local freeze campaigns, and the moral discussions led by the churches helped the freeze gain public attention. The issue was also kept in the public eye through political action. The freeze was first placed on the ballot as an issue to be voted on in western Massachusetts.

Early in 1980 Randall Kehler was teaching school in a small town in western Massachusetts. He and others had founded the Traprock Peace Center in Deerfield, Massachusetts, and they decided to try out the freeze idea on the voters. Along with the Northhampton Friends, they launched a campaign to put the issue on the ballot in November. If voters said yes to a freeze, the three state senators from western Massachusetts would be instructed to introduce a resolution in the state senate. The resolution would call on the President to propose to the Soviet Union that both countries adopt the freeze.

Their method was certainly a roundabout way of influencing the President, but it was a good test of voter opinion. Volunteers stood in front of supermarkets explaining the freeze idea and gathering signatures on petitions to put the freeze on the ballot. Once that was achieved, they began preparing brochures and educational materials, organizing study groups and house meetings, showing films, raising money for ads on tv and radio, and gaining endorsements from government leaders.

The volunteers found surprising support. "We discovered that most people really *are* against nuclear weapons and nuclear war," the organizers said. The freeze was endorsed by moderate to conservative newspapers and by Republican Congressman Silvio Conte. Ordinary citizens expressed their fears about nuclear war on radio and tv ads. In newspaper ads, health-care professionals emphasized the medical consequences of nuclear war; human services providers talked about the effects of military spending on local services; the local Council of Churches discussed the religious and ethical implications; and local businesspeople discussed the merits of the moratorium itself.

When the voters chose in November 1980, 59 percent said yes, they wanted a freeze. The vote did not gain much national attention, but peace groups knew they had a winning idea. Even in the thirty-three towns where a majority of the people voted for President Reagan, thirty of the towns also voted for the freeze.

Like a true grass-roots movement, local freeze campaigns started to spring up simultaneously. Just over the Massachusetts border, in Vermont, 18 towns considered the freeze in their annual town meetings in March 1981. All 18 meetings passed it. A year later, when they met again, 152 more Vermont towns passed the freeze, as did 50 in New Hampshire, 55 in Maine, 25 in Massachusetts, and 4 in Connecticut. One poster devised by the campaign proclaimed on a background of snow, "A nuclear freeze begins in town meetings."

The political goal of the freeze campaign in 1981 was to persuade government representatives to endorse and work for adoption of the freeze as a national policy objective. The strategy was to build support from the ground up, rather than going to national leaders directly. Volunteers gathered more than two and a half million signatures on freeze petitions to demonstrate to public officials how much support the idea had. A Harris poll in April 1982 found 81 percent of the public in favor of a freeze.

Once government representatives seemed convinced, freeze organizers asked city councils, more town meetings, and state legislatures to put the matter to a vote. By 1983 a freeze resolution had passed 446 New England town meetings, 361 city councils, 68 county councils, and one or both houses of 23 state legislatures—Massachusetts, Oregon, New York, Connecticut, Maine, Minnesota, Vermont, Wisconsin, Kansas, Iowa, Maryland, Hawaii, Delaware, Washington, Pennsylvania, California, Alaska, Illinois, Ohio, West Virginia, Missouri, North Carolina, and New Mexico.

Another way to generate debate was to put the freeze on state ballots as an initiative, an opportunity for voters to vote on an issue. In California a businessman, Harold Willens, launched a campaign to put the freeze on the California ballot in November 1982. In six months volunteers collected 600,000 signatures, twice more than needed to put it on the ballot. Similar campaigns occurred in nine other states and the District of Columbia. Thirty percent of the American people would have a chance to vote on the freeze in the November 1982 elections.

Nineteen eighty-two was a big year for the freeze campaign. As it gathered local and state support, a national political campaign was organized. On March 10, 1982, Senators Hatfield and Kennedy introduced a resolution advocating a moratorium on the testing, production, and deployment of nuclear weapons and then negotiations to reduce the number of weapons possessed by the two superpowers. A similar measure was introduced in the House by Representatives Edward J. Markey and Silvio Conte of Massachusetts, and Jonathan Bingham of New York.

The momentum of the freeze movement was rapidly exceeding the hopes even of those coordinating it. A clearinghouse set up by the national freeze campaign in St. Louis, Missouri, was deluged with requests for information. Freeze campaigns were started in 43 states and 279 congressional districts. By 1983 campaigns existed in all 50 states, with about 650 local freeze organizations. Groups not directly involved in the freeze movement, like the Wilderness Society and the National Organization for Women, began to support it.

To celebrate the growth of public consciousness, several large rallies were held in the spring of 1982, some coinciding with the United Nations Second Special Session on Disarmament. About 85,000 people listened to rock music and prayed in support of the session in the Rose Bowl in Pasadena. The biggest rally was in New York City, where more than 700,000 people gathered in Central Park, the largest political rally in American history.

In the House of Representatives the resolution gained support so quickly a vote was taken in August. The freeze lost by only two votes, 204 to 202. That narrow margin of defeat encouraged volunteers to work even harder for the November elections.

The freeze campaign itself did not raise money to help defeat Representatives who had voted against the freeze. But other groups did. A new political action committee was formed by the Council for a Livable World to raise money for House candidates. The U.S. Committee Against Nuclear War, founded by nine Congressmen, also raised funds to support congressional candidates who support the freeze.

When the dust settled after the November 1982 elections, the freeze came out a clear winner. Sixty percent of those who had a chance to vote on it approved the call for a freeze. The freeze passed in nine of the ten states where it was on the ballot (only Arizona voted no) and in the District of Columbia.

Voters of differing political views seemed to support it, from California, where the Reagan Administration had

Disarmament demonstrators lie in front of the United States Mission in New York in the summer of 1982. The United Nations building is in the background.

worked hard to defeat it, to solid Republican Suffolk County in New York. It passed in industrial states, western states, northern plains states, rural areas, and in large metropolitan areas like Chicago and Miami. Twelve congressional opponents of the freeze resolution were defeated. Eleven of the seventeen candidates supported by the United States Committee Against Nuclear War won.

The public expression of support made an impression on Congress. After a national call-in and a Citizens' Lobby, the freeze resolution passed the House by a vote of 278–149 in March 1983. Opponents had delayed the vote for a month by proposing numerous amendments. One that was approved changed the wording of the resolution to include reductions negotiated within a reasonable period of time. Since freeze advocates had always intended for reductions to follow a freeze, they claimed a victory.

The resolution's chances of being passed by the Senate, where thirty-three of one hundred Senators have sponsored it, seem slimmer. Supporting Senators hope at least to have the freeze debated in the Senate.

THE FUTURE OF THE FREEZE

As the freeze passed the House, freeze advocates were looking ahead to the next steps. If the freeze passes the Senate, too, it is nonbinding on the President. It merely calls on him to change the objective of the arms talks to "deciding when and how to achieve a mutual verifiable freeze," and then negotiate reductions. Because President Reagan has been doggedly opposed to the freeze, it seems unlikely he would carry it out.

What the freeze campaign really wants is a change in policy. Even as the freeze resolution is debated, supporters are also trying to stop the new MIRVed ICBMs of the United States and the Soviet Union. They hope to put a lid on the arms race until the 1984 elections.

The freeze campaign hopes for a new President in 1984. Randall Forsberg stated, "If we expect to have a freeze, we need to have a new government." A political action committee (PAC), independent of the freeze campaign, was set up for supporters who want to influence the election. They may try to collect statements from ten to eleven million voters that they won't support a candidate who doesn't support the freeze. Reagan's advisers have told him an arms treaty would be half of what he needs for re-election. (The other half is economic recovery.)

The rapid growth of the freeze movement took the country by surprise. Randall Kehler, who had become the national coordinator, had an explanation: "Because the bilateral freeze is so inherently clear and comprehensible, because it makes so much common sense, it is winning the support of a wide spectrum of American people."

Unlike previous peace movements, the freeze movement was not limited to students or pacifists. Support came from all ages, all occupations, both major parties, and most religions. Clearly, from the village square had come America's voice. Claimed one national staffperson, "People power is our strongpoint." The freeze movement was democracy in action.

DICK VAUGHAN

Dick Vaughan organized a freeze campaign in Kearney, Nebraska, a city of twenty thousand people halfway across the state on I-80. Vaughan was the Director of Religious Education at Kearney State College, having retired from the active priesthood when he married in 1972.

"I knew I had to do something," Vaughan said, when he came back from a freeze conference in Denver in 1982. His motivation was primarily religious and moral. He was affected by Einstein's reflection after the atom bomb: "The unleashed power of the atom has changed everything save our modes of thinking, and we thus drift toward unparalleled catastrophe." So he put something together on the freeze for the parish council and "got a reaction."

At that time Nebraskans were 78 percent against the freeze and 22 percent for it, according to the calculations of the national freeze campaign. Vaughan was gung ho to put the freeze on the state ballot as an initiative, but freeze supporters lacked organization or enough volunteers for a statewide campaign. So a small group decided to try it out on the municipal elections ballot in Kearney.

Their campaign met some resistance—one billboard was cut down repeatedly and "we kept repainting it," but mainly people didn't take the campaign seriously. "People didn't even want to bring up the subject; we had kind of a shell over us. We disturbed a quiet little town that doesn't like confrontation and conflict."

One of the turning points of the campaign was a talk by a Hiroshima survivor who related her experience. Her account, given at the Lutheran chapel on the state college campus, "was a beautiful experience" for the listeners.

Another boost to the campaign came from the Kearney Ministerial Association, which voted 3 to 1 to support the freeze in the months before the ballot vote. "That was a real surprising affirmation in a conservative community," Vaughan said.

The freeze won in Kearney by 57 votes, 50.4 percent to 49.6 percent. The triumph was low-key. "I don't know if we took a vote today," Vaughan said in the spring of 1983, "whether we'd win or not." But there were individual victories. A friend who had spent twenty-two years in nuclear forces in Europe revealed to Vaughan after the election, "I voted for the freeze."

4

WHAT IS A NUCLEAR WEAPONS FREEZE?

A nuclear weapons freeze means calling a halt to the production, testing, and deployment of nuclear weapons. It's a time-out in the arms race, a cooling-off period, a cease-fire during which both sides look at how they might solve their problems differently.

Imagine yourself in a two-person race. Every time you pull ahead, the person behind you speeds up to catch up with you and stay even. You go faster to try to shake him, but he catches up again.

Or imagine that you are behind in the race and every time you pull even, the other person sprints ahead, so that soon you are running faster and faster, using more and more strength and concentration just to stay even, but no one is winning.

At least, that's what you *think* is happening, but you're not sure because you can't really see the other person all the time, and he has cheerleaders who exaggerate his progress and make it sound as if he's pulling ahead. You're afraid that if you don't keep running you'll lose the race and be killed—those are the rules—but if you win the race, you may die anyway—that's the catch.

How can you stop the race without either person being killed?

Someone could wave a white flag when the runners are about even and declare the race a tie (even if photos show one slightly ahead). Both runners could freeze in place and then argue about who won. That is the solution offered by the freeze. It would break the deadly momentum of the arms race by simply saying "stop."

Two words are important when talking about the freeze. They are "mutual" and "verifiable." Freeze advocates say that both the United States and Russia should agree to a freeze and the freeze should be verifiable. Each country should know that the other is not producing new weapons.

WHAT DOES THE FREEZE COVER?

---

(1) The freeze would suspend underground nuclear testing, pending a final agreement on a comprehensive test ban treaty.

(2) The freeze would stop the testing, production, and deployment of all missiles and new aircraft whose main or sole payload is nuclear weapons. For the United States, this would stop cruise missiles, Trident I and II submarine-launched ballistic missiles, the improved Minuteman and MX intercontinental ballistic missiles, the Pershing 2 intermediate-range ballistic missile, and a new bomber like the B-1.

For the Soviet Union, it would put a halt to the SS-19 ICBM and SS-17, SS-18, SS-19 ICBM improvements; the SS-N-18 and SS-N-20 SLBMs; the SS-20 intermediate-range missile, and the Backfire bomber. The newest bombers capable of carrying nuclear weapons, missiles, and low-flying cruise missiles of both countries would be stopped. Each would keep what it has already produced. Missiles and aircraft could be maintained indefinitely by replacing parts.

(3) The number of land- and submarine-based launch tubes for nuclear missiles would be frozen. Replacement submarines could be built but with no new missiles or additional launch tubes.

(4) No more warheads (bombs) could be added to existing missiles or bombers.

(5) The freeze would halt the production of fissionable material (the enriched uranium and plutonium used to make bombs).

(6) The production of warheads would be stopped.

HOW WOULD THE
FREEZE COME ABOUT?

The freeze will come about when public support forces the leaders of both countries to announce a freeze. The freeze movement hopes to turn public opinion into a new public policy. The resolution passed by the House provides that a freeze would be negotiated, not merely proclaimed. The objective of the current arms control talks would become deciding "when and how to achieve a mutual verifiable freeze."

When a freeze is announced, the main elements of the proposal could begin immediately while negotiators work out the details of a treaty. After a detailed moratorium has been agreed upon, both countries could then begin negotiating to reduce the stockpiles of weapons, missiles, bombers, and submarines they now have.

Some peace advocates urge reductions of as much as 50 percent, but the freeze campaign has set no specific figure. Eventually the remaining nuclear arsenals could be dismantled.

CAN WE TRUST
THE RUSSIANS?

A key element of the freeze is verification. One of the most frequent objections made to the freeze is: We can't trust the Russians to abide by it. How could we be sure they wouldn't cheat?

The answer given by freeze supporters is: We don't have to trust the Russians. William Colby, former head of the CIA, testified before the Senate Foreign Affairs Committee, "We do not have to nor should we 'trust' the Russians," because a freeze can be satisfactorily verified. By using national technical means—satellites, radar, underwater detecting devices, on-land listening posts—we could detect any major activity in violation of a freeze. Both the Soviet Union and the United States agreed during the SALT talks that each had adequate means to monitor the other side's compliance with treaties.

We would have no trouble detecting whether the Soviet Union is producing new missiles, aircraft, or submarines. Satellite-based cameras now cover every inch of the U.S.S.R., with enough accuracy to read a license plate in Moscow. The cameras can zoom in on anything suspicious and produce an ultra-detailed photograph. We can see missile silos, launch-control systems, bombers on the ground, submarines in port, air, and naval bases, factories, submarine construction yards, and the highways and railroads leading into and out of plants. We know that the Russians have 134 major final assembly plants for nuclear arms, over 3,500 individual installations that provide support, 37 plants that produce aircraft material, and 49 that produce missile material. All of them could be watched.

The testing of missiles and weapons can be detected, too, by satellite photographs, seismic devices, and space-based sensors. Both the United States and the U.S.S.R.

can verify a nuclear explosion as small as 1 kiloton in any environment.

Detecting the production of warheads and fissionable materials (the fifth and sixth parts of a freeze) would be harder. On-site inspection—going into the country and actually checking a plant or missile in person—is the most reliable method. In the past the Russians have been reluctant to allow such inspections, but they seem to be modifying their position. During negotiations for a Comprehensive Test Ban Treaty in 1978, they agreed to allow ten seismic stations—black boxes—on Russian soil. The boxes would record every Soviet test of nuclear weapons. Other evidence the Russians are changing their position came from a Soviet diplomat who said, "The more comprehensive the substance of the treaty in question, the greater degree of on-site inspection we would agree to."

Though less reliable than on-site inspection, national technical means can also detect activity at plants that make warheads. Under a freeze, any activity at plants that make warheads would be suspicious. In the United States, nuclear warheads are put together at only three plants—Rocky Flats near Denver, Colorado; in Oak Ridge, Tennessee, and near Amarillo, Texas. Only a few plants make warheads in Russia, too, and they were identified in the 1970s. Closing down the plants after a freeze could be monitored by satellite. Any further activity at the plants, such as railroad cars or trucks leaving or entering, would be noticed. Once missile and nuclear-capable aircraft construction stopped, there would be little need for more warheads.

A freeze on the production of fissionable materials—plutonium and enriched uranium—is more difficult to verify. In countries that have promised not to make a bomb, the International Atomic Energy Commission Agency already uses on-site inspections and tamper-proof cameras to see that plutonium and enriched uranium are not removed from the nuclear power plants and reprocessed to make nuclear bomb fuel. Even without such measures, activity at plants that produce plutonium and enriched uranium could be detected. The cooling towers of plutonium plants release detectable heat, for example.

Some of the new weapons present verification difficulties, too. The cruise missile is highly mobile and relatively small, making it harder to detect. It looks like a torpedo. A satellite would not be able to tell if it was indeed carrying a nuclear warhead. On-site inspection would be necessary.

Absolute verification would probably not be possible. We won't be 100 percent sure nothing new is happening, but it is very unlikely the Soviets would be able to surprise us with a secret superweapon. Nuclear weapons or delivery systems take ten years to develop and go through five stages: research, development, testing, production, and deployment. Detection can occur at any stage. The Pentagon knew in 1982, for example, that the Russians were about to test two new missiles that would use solid rather than liquid fuel. The missiles were discovered at the research and development stage.

In addition to verification, some amount of trustworthiness would be necessary for a freeze to work. The Soviet Union has shown that it will abide by the letter of arms control treaties. According to our Department of State, the Soviets have abided by the 1963 Partial Test Ban Treaty, the 1967 ban on nuclear weapons in outer space, the SALT agreements of 1974 and the Anti-Ballistic Missile Treaty, and the unratified SALT II agreements of 1979. The two superpowers have signed fourteen arms control agreements and neither has violated them.

Both countries would have other reasons to adhere to a freeze. Any weapons developed in secret would have no value as a deterrent. If either country decided to develop a weapon in secret, it would risk a loss of international prestige if detected.

By and large, the opposition to a freeze is more political than technical. Those insisting on on-site inspection are often using verification as an obstacle because they are opposed to the arms control treaties themselves. William Colby feels verification is not the real problem: if violations are of the magnitude that would threaten us, they would be evident.

The Reagan Administration arms control negotiator, Paul Nitze, has testified that verification is not "an absolute requirement, it is a means toward the end of a good agreement. If those provisions of an agreement which are strategically significant to us are adequately verifiable, the agreement might be a good agreement, even if its less important provisions are not confidently verifiable."

Moreover, one must weigh the risk of violations against the risk of nuclear war. A poll taken by the *Washington Post* and ABC News found that six out of seven Americans believe the Soviet Union would secretly violate a nuclear freeze, but the majority of them still favor a freeze.

WHAT EFFECT WOULD THE FREEZE HAVE ON OUR NATIONAL ECONOMY?

There are two contradictory views toward military spending. One says the defense of our country is so important it overrides any economic considerations. If we don't spend enough on the military, we'll be taken over by other countries and it won't matter how much we have to spend on anything else.

This view was explicit in Secretary of Defense Caspar Weinberger's statement to Congress, when he was urging a 10 percent increase (over inflation) to the 1984 defense budget. "It's absolutely necessary that we continue [large military budgets] because it will take us a good five years to regain the strategic and conventional strength and readiness that I think we need to be able to assure the American people that we still have a very credible and effective deterrent."

The other view says a large percentage of the money we spend on defense is unnecessary. This view assumes we have "enough" defense and that more weapons won't buy more security. Spending less on defense and more on peace-related activities would make nuclear war less likely. More money would be available for human services like food stamps, housing, and health care.

Pope Paul VI stated this view in 1976. Military build-up, he said, "is an act of aggression which amounts to a crime, for even when they are not used, by their cost alone, armaments kill the poor by causing them to starve."

How much are we actually spending on defense? Much more than we used to. In 1939 the United States spent $1.1 billion on defense. In 1982 defense spending was about $183 billion. Defense spending absorbs a large part of the federal budget. The fiscal year 1982 budget allotted 56 percent to the military and payment for past wars. This includes veterans benefits and interest on the national debt, much of which was incurred for wars.

In forecasting his budgets for each of his four years as President between 1981 and 1984, Ronald Reagan has asked for $30 billion to $40 billion cuts in social programs and $30 billion to $40 billion increases in military spending. Over a five-year period he proposed to spend $1.6 trillion on defense. These priorities earned his spending plan a label—the New Militarism. An average family of four will pay the government $19,000 in taxes to finance its share of $1 trillion in defense.

The nuclear weapons programs are not a large part of the defense budget. The largest part of the defense budget goes for salaries and pensions. Some $44 billion went for nuclear programs in 1982, less than a fourth of the defense budget.

A nuclear weapons freeze would save the U.S. economy about $22 billion a year, half of what is now spent on nuclear programs. Although the savings would be smallest in the first year of a freeze (about $6 billion), they would increase rapidly after that. The estimated savings over the next five years would be $84 billion.

The planned nuclear programs that would not be affected by a freeze (such as new communications systems, ballistic missile defense, and new bomber defenses) might prove unnecessary and could also be reduced. If that happens, the savings would be well over $200 billion over the next decade.

The adverse impact of a freeze on military jobs would not be as severe as might be expected because most military employees work in conventional rather than nuclear weapons. One estimate says about 315,000 jobs would be lost if a freeze is implemented in fiscal year 1986. The freeze answer to the potential loss of jobs is conversion: the government-aided conversion of nuclear industries to producing civilian products.

Although the savings from a freeze would be only a part of the defense budget, any savings from defense would have a positive effect on the economy. The military employs a large number of people, but military spending does not create as many jobs as an equal amount of civilian spending would. For example, one billion dollars spent on education creates 187,299 jobs; on health care, 138,939 jobs; on construction, 100,072; on mass transit, 92,071; on the military, only 75,710 (Bureau of Labor Statistics).

One billion dollars spent on the MX missile program puts about 17,000 people to work. The same $1 billion would put 48,000 hospital workers in jobs, 65,000 people in the building trades to work, or hire 77,000 teachers, police or firefighters. The cost of the B-1 bomber program nearly matches all the money allocated by Congress for job training in the past twenty years.

Military spending contributes to inflation. Billions of

dollars' worth of weapons just sit in arsenals, becoming obsolete before they are used. They don't need many people to take care of them and they have no economic use. Cruise missiles don't need drivers nor can they be reused.

The production of weapons and missiles is also very costly. Only a few large corporations build them, so there is little competitive bidding for the contracts. Once production begins, the defense department has been very ineffective at controlling costs. The Navy's F-18 fighter plane, for example, now costs four times its original estimate to build. The M-1 tank costs seven times the original estimate.

Spending money on arms takes revenue away from other needs. The United States puts 20 percent of its scientists and engineers to work in military research and production. More than half of the money the United States spends for research and development goes to military research and development. (Japan spends only 2 percent of such money on the military and Germany only 12 percent.) Disproportionate spending on the military slows down a country's overall economic growth. Japan, which spends only 0.9 percent of its gross domestic product on defense, experienced a growth rate twice that of the United States in the 1960s and 1970s.

The United States is not the only country that spends heavily on arms. The world spends $550 billion for military purposes. In thirty-two countries, governments spend more for the military than for education and health care combined. The savings from a freeze on nuclear weapons could help reduce inflation, balance budgets, reduce taxes, and create more jobs if shifted to human services.

President Eisenhower summed up the human cost of a continuing arms race: "Every gun that is made, every warship launched, every rocket fired, signifies, in the final sense, a theft from those who hunger and are not fed, those who are cold and not clothed. This world in arms is not spending money alone; it is spending the sweat of its laborers, the genius of its scientists, the hopes of its children."

To summarize, the following arguments for a freeze have been made: The freeze provides a common sense way to stop the arms race. A freeze would be mutual. We have the capability to verify a freeze, so we don't have to trust the Russians. And a freeze on nuclear weapons would be beneficial to the economy. In Chapter 5, we will see why freeze advocates feel a sense of urgency about enacting a freeze now.

PEACE PEDALLERS

At a New Year's retreat in 1981, a college student, Paul Jolly, told a meeting of Young Friends (Quakers) in California that he was thinking about taking a cross-country bike trip. He wanted to take a break from his studies at Sarah Lawrence College, try an experiment in community living, and somehow express his concern about the arms race. Registration for the draft had just been reinstated for 18-year-olds, and he felt he was being asked to put his signature on the preparation for war. Jolly's plan was to bicycle across the country in a caravan during the summer of 1982, stopping to talk with school and church groups about peace.

Caryn Daschbach said right away she'd like to go. Rick Shory, who was taking part in the Walk to Moscow, read about the bicycle caravan in a Friends newsletter and decided he'd rather pedal than walk. Jolly raised money during the summer of 1981 and contacted people to stay with across the country. Other young people joined, and by March 1982 six Peace Pedallers, three men and three women, struck out from San Francisco. Besides Jolly, Daschbach, and Shory, the Pedallers were Jonathan Vogel, Linda Kuckhahn, and Lauren Crutcher.

From the beginning, the trip and the plans for talking about peace were flexible. The Pedallers found the communal aspect of the trip as challenging as the peace persuading. "We divided the country and each person was responsible for planning our travel for different stretches of the trip," Jolly related, but at times they had six different goals.

Despite the fact that five of the six were Friends, they differed in their religious views and on whether the caravan should try to reach as many people as possible or demonstrate a peaceful community on the road. Nevertheless, they hung together for 6,000 zigzagging miles (9,656 km) from California to Washington, D.C., some dropping out periodically for other commitments and then returning.

Averaging about 200 miles (320 km) a week, or about five to eight hours of bicycling a day, the Pedallers spoke to about 200 Friends meetings and community gatherings. They stopped at Kearney, Nebraska, where they had a potluck picnic with Dick Vaughan and other freeze volunteers. They encountered many people who were frightened by the prospect of nuclear war, many who felt no responsibility to forestall it, and many who felt powerless to prevent it.

Paul remembered one seventh-grader who kept asking, "Why do we keep building more and more weapons if we can blow up the world already?"

"He really wanted to know," Paul recalled, "and I couldn't answer."

The caravan mailed six issues of a newsletter, *The Second Wind.* "It becomes clearer in every encounter that no one wants nuclear war and that ever-increasing numbers are open to the idea of disarmament," Paul wrote in the first issue.

In October, the Pedallers arrived without fanfare in Washington, D.C. Along the way they had asked children to draw pictures of what they thought peace was like. The Pedallers met with a staff member from the public relations office of the Arms Control Agency who promised to pass the pictures on to the White House. "He talked about numbers of missiles and we talked about the prayer in our hearts," Jolly said.

The Pedallers returned to their homes and studies, but they were changed people as a result of their experience. "We seem to be more deliberate about where we live, how we earn money, what our spiritual community is." Two are now writing a book about the summer, a time they took to live together peacefully and try "to slow the perpetual drift toward war."

5

THE TIME
IS NOW

Freeze advocates say there is no better time for a freeze than now. The time is right because a rough balance exists between the nuclear forces of the United States and the U.S.S.R. Such a balance—known as *parity*—has not existed before and may never exist again. The numbers of missiles, warheads, and bombers may not be exactly the same, but overall the two countries have the same power to destroy each other.

The 1982 U.S. Department of Defense Annual Report admitted this situation: "While the era of U.S. superiority is long past, parity—not U.S. inferiority—has replaced it, and the United States and the Soviet Union are roughly equal in strategic nuclear power." Parity is seen as the ideal context in which to negotiate a freeze. When neither side feels inferior, stability is more likely to result.

The problem is that not everyone agrees parity exists or if it does, that it is desirable. President Reagan claims the Soviet Union has a "definite margin of superiority" in nuclear weapons. The 1980 Republican presidential campaign platform called for the United States to attain nuclear superiority. When elected, Reagan initiated a plan to modernize our weapons in order to achieve that superiority.

PARITY

Does the Soviet Union have a margin of superiority? Comparisons are difficult to make because mere numbers do not always indicate strategic superiority. Although both countries have a triad defense—ground-launched missiles, bombers, and submarine-launched missiles— each country has different strengths. The Soviets have favored land-based missiles. With greater access to the oceans, the United States has favored submarine-based missiles.

In number of warheads, the superpowers are roughly comparable. The United States has 9,500 nuclear warheads; the Soviet Union about 7,700. The warhead count is the closest it has ever been since the arms race began.

Defense Secretary Caspar Weinberger said the number of warheads "is not a very accurate measure because it doesn't take into account the age, the accuracy or the yield" of such warheads. United States warheads are generally more accurate and the Soviet warheads have a higher explosive yield.

"Megatonnage, too, makes little difference," says former arms negotiator Paul Warnke. "The fact that they [the Soviets] might have a two-megaton warhead, compared to our modest ones of something like 400,000 tons of TNT, only makes one difference: how big is the hole going to be where the high school used to be?"

In delivery systems—land and submarine-based missiles and bombers—the two sides are also close. The Soviets have a slight edge: 2,500 to 2,000. A mere tally is misleading because some missiles are more vulnerable to

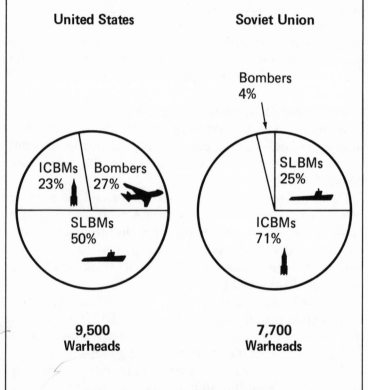

SUPERPOWERS'
STRATEGIC ARSENALS

United States

Soviet Union

Bombers
4%

ICBMs
23%

Bombers
27%

SLBMs
25%

SLBMs
50%

ICBMs
71%

9,500
Warheads

7,700
Warheads

Source: Union of Concerned Scientists.
The Arms Control Debate, Cambridge, MA: 1982.

enemy attack than others. Missiles deployed on the ground, usually in hardened cement containers called silos, are much more vulnerable than those on a submarine.

Fifty percent of the U.S. missiles are deployed on submarines; the Soviet Union deploys only 25 percent of their missiles on subs. Half of the American nuclear-armed subs are on patrol at any given time. The Soviet Union, with more limited access to the oceans, keeps only 15 percent on patrol. United States submarines are quieter and harder to detect; we also have more advanced antisubmarine technology.

The Russians have 71 percent of their missiles on the ground; the United States has 23 percent on the ground. Another 27 percent of U.S. warheads are on bombers, a third of which are constantly on alert. The Soviet Union has only 4 percent of its warheads on bombers.

Thus, in terms of missiles that could evade a nuclear attack and then be used to retaliate, the United States has an advantage. When General John Vessey, Chairman of the Joint Chiefs of Staff in the latter half of 1982, was asked if he would trade our armed forces for the Soviet Union's, he replied, "Not on your life."

Each country has its strengths and each side clearly has enough weapons to destroy the other. Using only 5 percent of their total available megatonnage, the Soviet Union could destroy all of our industry and urban population. We could do the same to them using 4 percent of our megatonnage.

President Reagan is most concerned about the Soviet advantage in land-based missiles, including the 250–275

Comparison of superpowers' arsenals shows great differences in basing of warheads.

intermediate-range missiles aimed at Europe and the improved accuracy and numbers of their MIRVed ICBMs. During his campaign he talked about a "window of vulnerability," which is a window in time. Our land-based missiles, such as the Minuteman and Titan, are highly vulnerable to a Soviet surprise attack, he claimed. By the mid-1980s the Soviet ICBMs will have enough accuracy and explosive power to destroy most of our ICBMs in their silos. Between then and the time it takes the United States to build an alternative system, we are vulnerable. Reagan's five-year military modernization program was to close this window.

Some defense analysts question whether there really is a serious problem. Even if the Russians attack first, enough ground-based missiles could be launched to destroy the Soviet Union. We would only need seven submarines or twenty B-52s or 15 percent of our ICBMs.

Warnke points out that the very vulnerability of land missiles was the reason we put two-thirds of our warheads on submarines and bombers. No foolproof way has yet been found to protect the ground-based missiles. "If we are vulnerable to Russian attack through a window, then they are vulnerable to our attack through a barn door," he said.

Much of the recent talk of a Soviet advantage comes from the decade of the 1970s when the Soviet Union modernized its strategic forces while the United States slowed its pace of defense spending. This decade is what freeze opponents refer to when they say: "A freeze would reward a persistent Soviet military buildup and penalize some 15 years of unilateral American restraint."

There is some controversy over what in fact the Soviets accomplished in the 1970s. Since 1962, it was thought, the Soviets had been increasing their military spending by about 3 percent a year above inflation. CIA specialists now say the rate was overestimated; it may have been no more than 2 percent. Whatever the rate, there is no question the Soviets spend heavily on arms. For many years they have invested 11 to 15 percent of their GNP (all the goods and services that are produced in a year) in the military. The United States invests about 7 percent of its GNP in the military.

The results of the spending provide a better basis of comparison, however. Former Secretary of Defense Harold Brown said the Soviets have come from "a position of substantial numerical inferiority fifteen years ago to one of parity today."

Despite this acknowledgment of parity, the talk of Soviet superiority persists. Presidents tend to bring up arms gaps when they are campaigning or defending their military budget requests to Congress. President Eisenhower talked of a bomber gap; President Kennedy of a missile gap; and President Reagan of the land-based missile gap. These gaps have always turned out to be exaggerated, but the public often believes them.

"There is an ingrained tendency among government officials to overstate Soviet military power, understate Soviet military problems, and understate United States and allied military power," said the Center for Defense Information, an independent organization that includes former government officials.

"The myth of Soviet nuclear superiority is one of the greatest myths ever perpetrated on the American people," commented a retired Navy admiral, Gene R. LaRocque. "The United States has been three to five years ahead of the Soviets in every missile system from the A and H bombs to the MIRVed and Cruise missiles."

Whether the Soviets are gaining on us or not, the United States is developing a whole new generation of weapons. Those weapons—the Trident II, the MX, the Pershing 2, and cruise missiles—lend urgency to the freeze movement. Once they are produced and deployed, say freeze supporters, the two countries will no longer be at parity. A hair-raising new round of the arms race will begin.

NEW WEAPONS

What are these new weapons? They are part of a $1.6 trillion defense spending plan President Reagan introduced for 1982–87. The amount requested more than doubled the defense budget in five years. Included in the plan approved by Congress was $180 billion for strategic modernization, improvements the President thought were needed to regain nuclear superiority.

The major parts of the buildup are:

(1) *Thousands of cruise missiles,* small, pilotless computerized jets, each carrying nuclear bombs fifteen times as powerful as the bomb dropped on Hiroshima. Cruise missiles can be deployed on bombers, ships, submarines, or on ground launchers. They can fly great distances at very low altitudes hidden from the enemy's radar and land within 100 feet (30.48 m) of their targets.

(2) *Seventeen thousand more warheads* to be produced in the next fifteen years.

(3) *One hundred MX missiles,* each capable of delivering ten warheads, with each warhead equal to twenty-five "Hiroshimas." The first forty MX missiles would be deployed in existing silos between 1985 and 1987 at a cost of $21.6 billion. Because of their greater accuracy and payload, they could destroy Soviet ICBMs in their silos. But because no good basing plan has been found, the MX missiles themselves would be vulnerable to a Soviet first strike.

(4) *MK-12A warheads* for the Minuteman III missiles. The 900 MK-12As will each have twice the accuracy and double the explosive power of the existing warheads on the Minuteman IIIs.

(5) *One hundred new B-1 bombers,* to replace B-52s. These long-range bombers will be able to carry nuclear bombs and cruise missiles or conventional bombs. Each costs between $300 and $400 million. The Carter Administration scrapped the original B-1 in favor of the cruise missiles, but Reagan proceeded with both cruise missiles and the B-1 and plans for a Stealth bomber.

The justification for the B-1 is that it will penetrate improving Soviet air defenses better than the B-52. But the B-1s may not be able to do that for many more years, either, so another new bomber, with Stealth technology to evade radar, will be developed in the 1990s. In the meantime, the B-1s could be used as launching platforms for cruise missiles, standing off as far as 1,000 miles (1,600 km) from Soviet borders.

(6) *At least 12 Trident submarines,* one to be completed every ten months, each costing $1.3841 billion. The first, the *Ohio,* went to sea in August 1982, followed by the *Michigan* and the *Florida* in 1983. Twenty to 22 are eventually planned for the Trident fleet, if Congress authorizes them all.

Each submarine will carry 24 new Trident II missiles; each missile has 10 to 14 warheads. Each warhead could have 150 kilotons of power. Thus, one Trident submarine will be able to destroy 240 to 336 different cities in the Soviet Union with a blast ten times that of the Hiroshima bomb. Just 5.2 percent of the fleet's warheads would effectively destroy the Soviet Union. Four stories high and nearly two football fields in length, the Trident submarine with Trident II missiles has been described as "the deadliest weapon system ever built."

(7) *Eight hundred neutron bombs,* to be deployed mainly in Europe. Each one costs $3 million. The neutron bomb kills all living things in its target but destroys fewer buildings than a regular nuclear bomb and gives off a lower amount of radioactive contamination. Neutron bombs would be placed in artillery shells to be used against tanks. These bombs had also been scrapped by the Carter administration.

(8) *Command and control improvements*, costing some $8 billion, to enhance the capacity for fighting a nuclear war.

(9) *One hundred and eight launchers for the Pershing 2 missiles*. (The number of missiles to be produced is secret, but it is estimated at 220.) The Pershing 2 is an intermediate-range missile like the Soviets' SS-20. When it is deployed in West Germany, it will be able to reach targets in the Soviet Union within six to eight minutes of firing. The Pershing 2 is four times more accurate than the MX but carries a smaller warhead. Because of its speed and accuracy, it poses a danger to Soviet leadership and command posts.

The Soviets are also modernizing. Their ICBMs—the SS-17, SS-18, and SS-19—are being armed with increasingly accurate warheads. The SS-20, an intermediate range missile, is mobile and can be moved from border to border. Three hundred and fifty-one of them are now aimed at Europe or Asia.

The Russians are testing new, large submarines, such as the Typhoon, and SLBMs to go with them. They are also developing a cruise missile with a range of 1,800 miles (2,897 km) which will be in operation by the mid-1980s. They may also have a new long-range bomber. Like the United States, the Russians are building weapons that are smaller, faster, more accurate, more flexible, and have a longer range.

The new weapons on both sides would be harder to verify in an arms control agreement or freeze. The mobile ICBMs will hardly stay in one place long enough to be counted. The cruise missiles, which are only 10 to 20 feet (3 to 6 m) long, look like torpedoes. They are easy to conceal and can be deployed almost anywhere. It is hard to tell if they carry nuclear warheads without an on-site inspection. Once these new weapons are in place, it would be more difficult to enforce a freeze.

NUCLEAR WARFIGHTING

Why build all these new weapons when we already have enough to destroy the earth several times over?

The new weapon systems are linked to a change in nuclear strategy. Until a few years ago, both the Soviet Union and the United States operated under a state of mutual assured destruction, appropriately called MAD. Each power knew that the other had enough to destroy it, so it would be madness to attack. Nuclear war has been avoided for thirty years.

MAD threatened to destroy civilian populations in retaliation for a nuclear attack—"You try that and you'll be sorry." Each side assumed that even after an attack, the other side would still have enough weapons to retaliate and kill "too many" people. Large cities are fairly easy targets to hit when bombs are fifteen times greater than those dropped on Japan. A nuclear war between the United States and Russia would kill as many as 250 million people in a single day.

For deterrence, defense planners emphasized having a diversity of nuclear weapons and delivery systems—a triad—in case one part of the triad was knocked out. Emphasis was also placed on protecting the retaliatory force—putting missiles on subs that can hide in the oceans and bombs on bombers that can evade an attack by taking off. Because no effective protection has been discovered for ground-based missiles, they are the most likely to be knocked out in a nuclear attack.

The Pentagon shifted away from mutual assured destruction in the late 1970s. They began planning weapons designed not just to deter a nuclear war but to fight one. Instead of retaliatory missiles that could destroy cities, the Pentagon began to build more accurate missiles that could knock out Soviet missiles in their silos before they could be launched. This shift of targets from cities and people (a countervalue strategy) to military targets is called a *counterforce strategy*. Counterforce weapons must be faster, more accurate, and carry multiple warheads so they can hit many targets at once in a surprise attack.

Some consider the implications of a counterforce strategy alarming. Under a counterforce attack, cities would no longer be the prime targets. Twenty million people would still die, however, if U.S. missile silos were the only targets. Most major cities contain at least one military target.

The characteristics of the counterforce weapons make them look like first-strike weapons, as if each country is intent on destroying all the other side's missiles first. Why build the MX, for example—when no way has been found to hide or defend them—unless you plan to fire them first? The Minuteman and Titan missiles would be quite sufficient for retaliation and would have as much chance of getting off the ground as the MX if the Soviets attacked first. The MX is a better offensive weapon because it is more accurate. It would be able to knock out Soviet missiles in their silos; that is not a retaliatory job.

The Trident II missiles will also have enough accuracy to threaten missile silos. They can come within 300 feet (91 m) of the target with 150-kiloton bombs. With the addition of MARVs (maneuvering re-entry vehicles), their navigation can be corrected in flight, essentially increasing their accuracy to zero error.

A former missile designer, Robert Aldridge, said that when the fleet of ten Trident submarines is fitted with Trident II missiles in the 1990s, the fleet could knock out all but 168 of the Soviets' 1,398 land-based ICBMs in a surprise first attack.

The Pershing 2 can reach the Soviet Union in six to eight minutes from Europe, a speed more suited to a surprise attack than to retaliation.

In addition to building first-strike weapons, the Pentagon began developing scenarios for actually fighting a nuclear war. People sit at computers in the Pentagon and try out various attack and response patterns. A Pentagon document leaked to *The New York Times* in the spring of 1982 set out the guidelines of a five-year plan to prepare for a "protracted and winnable nuclear war" with the Soviet Union. During a protracted war "decapitation strikes" were planned to knock out the Soviet leadership and military command. From thinking nuclear war is unwinnable, planners moved to thinking about how to win it.

LIMITED NUCLEAR WAR

A corollary to nuclear warfighting is the idea that a nuclear confrontation could be limited once it began. This assumption was made when James Schlesinger, the Secretary of Defense for Presidents Nixon and Ford, developed the policy of a flexible response. The idea was that the United States should be able to respond to a military threat at any level: conventional, tactical nuclear weapons, medium-range nuclear weapons, and finally intercontinental strategic nuclear weapons.

"You've got to be able to fight a nuclear war at all levels, small and large," Schlesinger said, "in order to prevent it from happening at all."

As part of maintaining a flexible response, the United States deployed thousands of battlefield nuclear weapons in Europe. Some are small enough to be carried in knapsacks and launched by mortars. NATO might use these nuclear weapons if they were necessary to repel an invasion by conventional Russian soldiers and tanks. NATO "reserves the right" to use nuclear weapons first in that situation.

The smaller nuclear weapons violate the concept of a *firebreak*—the definite break between conventional and nuclear weapons, like a path cleared to prevent a fire from spreading. If NATO were to use these small nuclear bombs to attack advancing Soviet tanks in an invasion of Europe, has a nuclear exchange begun? Would the Soviets feel "justified" in also using small nuclear weapons? The losing side in such a conflict might be tempted to launch the intermediate-range missiles both are deploying in Europe.

Preparing a flexible response assumed that once nuclear weapons were used, a nuclear confrontation could be contained and would not escalate. Many leaders seriously doubt that. Former Russian President Leonid Brezhnev warned: "If a nuclear war breaks out, whether it be in Europe or in any other place, it would inevitably and unavoidably assume a worldwide character. Such is the logic of the war itself and the character of present-day armaments and international relations. . . . So those who possibly hope to set fire to the nuclear powder keg while themselves sitting snugly aside should not entertain any illusion."

American strategists have publicly backed off from the idea of fighting either a protracted or a limited nuclear war. Secretary of Defense Weinberger admitted there is no justification for the idea that nuclear war can be won and it is unlikely such a war could be protracted. A nuclear war, it has been said, would be fought not in the trenches but in an afternoon.

General David Jones, Chairman of the Joint Chiefs of Staff in the first half of 1982, said he had serious doubts as to whether any nuclear exchange could be prevented from escalating to an all-out war. Much of our defense strategy is still planned, however, around fighting rather than deterring nuclear war.

COULD WE SURVIVE?

As people became skeptical about limiting a nuclear war, they also became skeptical about civil defense. When President Reagan proposed his defense modernization plan, he also launched an ambitious civil defense plan. The plan admitted that 42 million people would die in an all-out nuclear war, but it claimed that 80 percent of the population could survive if evacuated to host areas or fallout shelters.

T. K. Jones, a defense official, claimed that nuclear war is survivable. "Dig a hole, cover it with a couple of doors and then throw three feet of dirt on top. . . . It's the dirt that does it. . . . If there's enough shovels to go around, everybody's going to make it."

The evacuation plan assumed a three-day warning of a nuclear attack. Every local community, under the direction of the Federal Emergency Management Agency (FEMA), was to adopt an emergency evacuation plan. Each region in the country was classified as to whether it was a "high risk area"—a target—or a host area for refugees.

Some host areas, like eastern Washington State, were later reclassified as targets themselves, leaving western Washington without much of a host. Two-thirds of the country's population, unfortunately, happens to live in and around designated risk areas. Nevertheless, in 30 million FEMA handbooks, evacuation routes were drawn up, model fallout shelters designed, and instructions given for what to do with pets in case of nuclear attack. (Leave them with enough food and water for a few days!)

Hundreds of local governments simply refused to cooperate. New York City's Council said planning to move ten million New Yorkers up to the Catskills was "voodoo preparedness." It was quite obvious to the average person that in the event of a nuclear war you might run but you can't hide. The "potential victims" joined the nuclear debate instead.

HAIR-TRIGGER READINESS

If civil defense plans elicited skepticism, the new weapons produced anxiety. Because missiles like the Pershing 2 could attack so quickly, they force the superpowers into a hair-trigger state of readiness. Their short attack time leaves only a few minutes for national leaders to decide whether the warning of an attack is a mistake to be ignored or a real attack to be retaliated against.

We have already had some near misses. In the mid-1960s the new Ballistic Missile Early Warning System (BMEWS—bemuse?) indicated that an all-out missile attack on the United States was occurring. Actually what the radar had seen was the rising of the moon!

During one eighteen-month period, 151 false alarms occurred, four of them serious enough to put bomber crews on the alert. Some of the kinks have been worked out of the system, but another false alarm occurred in June 1980 because of a "faulty integrated circuit in a communications multiplexer," a 46-cent computer chip.

The most serious false alarm occurred on November 9, 1979, when B-52 bomber crews and ICBMs were placed on alert for six minutes before an apparent Soviet attack was discovered to be a mistake. Three squadrons of planes with nuclear weapons took off so as not to be caught sitting on an airfield. A Pentagon technician had mistakenly put a war-games training tape of a Soviet attack on a military computer, which thought it was real. The President was to have been alerted at minute 7, but he couldn't be found. The six minutes required to detect this mistake would not have been available if Pershing 2 had been headed for Moscow from Europe.

In calm periods, there is time to make a rational decision about whether or not to counterattack. In a time of international crisis, however, the Russians particularly would be forced into a "use 'em or lose 'em" situation, since more than 70 percent of their missiles are on the ground and vulnerable to a surprise attack. They would have to decide whether to launch a counterattack in moments of incredible tension. Or they might be tempted to simply install a launch-on warning system, in which computers would automatically launch missiles in retaliation if they detected an attack. Former CIA analyst Arthur Macy Cox has warned that "nuclear weapons technology is rapidly advancing to the point where it can no longer be controlled by humans."

Conversely, the United States, with 50 percent of its missiles on submarines, would not feel as much pressure to hit while the hitting is good because the subs are likely to remain invulnerable to detection for many years to come.

Few Americans believe the United States would initiate a nuclear war, but the Russians do. Air Force General Lew Allen told Congress in 1981 that first-strike weapons like the MX would be devastating to the Russians. "They have to consider a U.S. first strike whether we think we would do that or not." The MX looks like a first-strike weapon to them, "designed not for deterrence but for launching the first strike and waging a nuclear war," said Allen. If both sides are soon able to launch an effective first strike, the stability of the planet rests on such perceptions of intent.

Thus the weapons stand poised across from each other, with new, more accurate, more powerful ones being produced every day. For these reasons, freeze advocates say a freeze is urgent:

(1) The United States and the Soviet Union are at a state of rough parity in nuclear forces which may not be achieved again soon.

(2) The freeze would prevent the deployment of a new generation of first-strike weapons. Once deployed, these weapons will establish a state of hair-trigger readiness which will greatly increase the risk of nuclear war in an international crisis. They will also be harder to verify.

(3) Neither a limited nor a protracted nuclear war is winnable or survivable.

"This is the moment," said Jesse Chiang, a peace candidate who opposed the late Senator Henry Jackson in Washington State. "If we miss it, it will not come back. Without the freeze, we are finished."

AMARILLO AND
THE PANTEX PLANT

A nuclear weapons freeze is not a popular idea in Amarillo, Texas. Amarillo is a city of 150,000 people in the panhandle area, the chimney that sticks up between Oklahoma and New Mexico. The largest private employer in Amarillo is the Pantex Plant, the final assembly point for all U.S. nuclear warheads. Each day, barbershop talk has it, three H-bombs or warheads leave Pantex by boxcar or truck to be shipped to their storage or deployment points. Some are fitted on Trident submarines in Bangor, Washington. Others may go on cruise missiles or on Minuteman II missiles.

The Pantex plant is 17 miles (27 km) out of town on 9,100 dusty acres (3,600 ha) of prairie scrub, in one of the most tornado-prone areas of the country. The concrete bunkers of the plant are surrounded by two 8-foot (2.44-m) fences topped with barbed wire, electronic sensors, and guard towers. A Texas poet has called Pantex "the factory where the end of the world begins."

Pantex is owned by the United States Government, operated by the Department of Energy, and managed by a private contractor, Mason & Hanger-Silas Mason Co., of Lexington, Kentucky. It employs 2,400 people in jobs both professional and nontechnical. The plant has always made weapons—conventional munitions during World War II, then nuclear weapons beginning in 1951. It has always been accepted by Amarillo as a necessary part of American defense.

Any concern about the work at Pantex was mostly unstated until the local bishop, Leroy T. Matthiesen, opened up the subject in a diocesan newsletter in September 1981. He called for an end to the arms race and urged "individuals involved in the production and stockpiling of nuclear weapons . . . to resign from such activities, and to seek employment in peaceful pursuits." Bishop Matthiesen had not been a supporter of antiwar activism before then, but he was changed by speaking to a priest who was jailed after a protest at the plant in the spring of 1981.

After Matthiesen's outspoken peace stand, "60 Minutes" came to Amarillo to film a segment on the issue of building nuclear weapons. Amarillo became a symbol of the polarizing trends in the country, said Presbyterian minister Dr. James R. Carroll, between the advocates for a nuclear weapons freeze and those who believe the presence of nuclear weaponry is the best guarantor of a peaceful world.

Since the events of 1981 and 1982, people in Amarillo are talking about the issue more, but the voters remain politically conservative and the "public peace people" number only ten to fifteen. Most of the churches give at least tacit support to the work at Pantex. The Reverend J. Alan Ford, minister at Southwest Baptist Church, an independent Baptist church, is definitely antifreeze. Southwest Baptist had a Pantex Appreciation Day, a patriotic rally in the church on a Sunday morning in May 1982.

"I don't believe there can be any such thing as a verifiable freeze with the Russians," Reverend Ford said. "Russia's already broken seventeen agreements with us. All you have to do is look at Afghanistan to see that Russia is not going to keep any agreement that is not to their advantage. We're dealing with an immoral government there."

No one likes weapons and no one likes war, he maintained, but nuclear weapons are a necessary part of defense, and it would be immoral to be unable to defend ourselves. Reverend Ford said that 95 percent of the city feels this way and that the freeze is not even a point of contention.

Dr. Carroll called himself a "dove with talons," who was very much for peace but did not see the call for a freeze as the wisest policy in the context of the world situation. The First Presbyterian Church has a peacemaking and peace-keeping task group whose purpose is educational. The group includes people with varying points of view. The freeze has been discussed by church members but no official stand has been taken. Dr. Carroll described the 2,000 members of his congregation as "very intelligent, thoughtful, informed people who see several sides to the issue." The United Campus Ministry sponsored a discussion of alternate paths to peace between Bishop Matthiesen and Dr. Winfred Moore of First Baptist Church, which Dr. Carroll cited as the type of thoughtful approach that has been taken.

"The nuclear freeze is an issue in other places. It's not an issue here at all," maintained City Commissioner David Taylor. Although his stand has had more national than local impact, Bishop Matthiesen felt it was important that the issue has been raised.

6

OPPOSITION TO
THE FREEZE

The opposing idea to a nuclear weapons freeze is peace through strength. Advocates of peace through strength say the national strategy of the United States should be "based on an overall military and technological superiority over the Soviet Union." Only from such a position of American strength can peace come.

The United States does not now have a clear superiority in nuclear weapons, so a military buildup would be necessary to achieve this strength. "It is time for us to start a buildup," said President Reagan as he began his administration, "and it's time for us to build to the point that no other nation on this earth will ever dare raise a hand against us, and in this way we will preserve world peace."

Peace-through-strength advocates believe the Soviets are intent on dominating the world unless the United States stops them. "The rulers in the Kremlin are as eager as Hitler was to get power over the whole world, but unlike Hitler they are not gamblers," said Edward Teller, the "father" of the hydrogen bomb. "If we can put up a missile defense that makes their attack dubious, chances are they will never try the attack. We can avoid a third world war but only if strength is in the hands of those who want peace more than they want power."

President Reagan likewise has taken a dim view of the Russians. Halfway through his administration, as he was pushing for a large increase in the defense budget, he told a national group of evangelical ministers that the Russians are evil incarnate. The two superpowers, he said, are locked in a "struggle between right and wrong, good and evil."

Some hawks (strong supporters of the military) feel there can never be peace until the Soviet system collapses, either through revolution, internal collapse, or external force. Until that happens the rest of the world would be "better dead than red."

These views are shared by several national organizations. The American Security Council has a political action arm known as the Coalition for Peace Through Strength. One hundred and twenty-five national organizations are part of the coalition, including the Veterans of Foreign Wars and the American Legion Auxiliary.

Some religious leaders also support a stronger nuclear defense. Catholic writer Michael Novak defends the value of nuclear weapons as a deterrent. Deterrence will not be effective, he says, without the will to use the weapons. Deterrence has a moral effect—the prevention of nuclear war. He has called the bishops who favor the freeze the war bishops, because their views are more likely to lead to war, he contends.

When Reagan was elected, the views of the peace-through-strength advocates became the dominant view in the national government. The Committee on the Present Danger was formed in March 1976 by Eugene Rostow, Paul Nitze, and James Schlesinger to influence public opinion about the dangers of detente and the need to increase military power. Many of the members of the Committee on the Present Danger became members of Reagan's cabinet. Paul Nitze was appointed his chief arms negotiator and Eugene Rostow, the head of the Arms Control and Disarmament Agency.

Other long-time hawks like the late Senator Henry Jackson of Washington, Richard Perle, once Jackson's assistant but now Assistant Secretary of Defense, and Zbigniew Brzezinski, former head of the National Security Council, all supported the peace through strength position.

With the backing of these individuals and groups, the Reagan Administration initiated a five-year military buildup. The same summer the freeze was first voted on in Congress, a peace-through-strength resolution was introduced. It was endorsed by 276 Congressional representatives, which was about 40 percent of Congress, before the 1982 elections. At least one house of 16 state legislatures also passed the resolution.

Peace through strength supporters opposed the freeze campaigns in the states and the freeze resolution pending in Congress. President Reagan suggested that the freeze movement was bent on "simple-minded appeasement or wishful thinking about our adversaries."

Instead of a freeze, President Reagan opened three different arms control talks:

(1) INF (Intermediate-range nuclear-forces talks) to reduce the number of intermediate-range missiles, particularly the Russian SS-20s and the American Pershing 2 and cruise missiles planned in Europe.

(2) START (Strategic-arms reduction talks) to reduce the number of long-range missiles and warheads the U.S. and U.S.S.R. each have. START is the successor to SALT II.

(3) MBFR (Mutual and balanced-force reductions talks) to reduce the conventional forces of the two countries.

The INF talks affect the defense of Europe. The countries in NATO (Belgium, Canada, Denmark, France, Greece,

**United States Special Representative for
Negotiations Edward L. Rowny and his Soviet
counterpart, Victor Karpov, shake hands prior to the
first plenary session of the Strategic Arms
Reduction Talks (START) in Geneva in June of 1982.**

Iceland, Italy, Luxembourg, the Netherlands, Norway, Portugal, Turkey, the United Kingdom, the United States, and West Germany) have not maintained armies and conventional weapons equal to those of the Warsaw Pact countries (the U.S.S.R., East Germany, Poland, Czechoslovakia, Rumania, Hungary, and Bulgaria). Instead NATO has relied on the "nuclear umbrella" of the United States. If Europe was suddenly invaded by the Soviets, NATO might use nuclear weapons to stop an advance. U.S. nuclear weapons have been in Western Europe since 1948 to deter such an attack.

When the Russians started deploying more than 300 new MIRVed intermediate-range missiles on European borders in 1979, NATO made a two-track decision: to deploy U.S. Pershing 2 and cruise missiles in Europe while beginning arms control talks to reduce both NATO and Soviet missiles. The INF talks resulted from the second part of that decision.

When the INF talks began in November 1981, the United States proposed a "Zero-Zero Option": the U.S. would cancel plans to deploy 108 Pershing 2 missiles and 464 ground-launched cruise missiles in Europe if the Soviets would withdraw and dismantle all of their intermediate-range missiles deployed on European borders, some 600 SS-20s and older SS-4s and SS-5s.

The Soviets counterproposed to reduce their intermediate-range missiles in Europe to 162, the total number of French and British missiles, if the United States forwent deployment. The United States rejected this offer on the ground that the French and British missiles are independent of NATO forces. Progress in the talks was very slow.

The Pershing 2 is the main threat to the Soviets because it could reach Moscow from Europe in only six minutes. The Americans are most concerned about the destructive power of the MIRVed missiles the Soviets are putting in place. One compromise suggested was for the United States to deploy cruise missiles, which would take two hours to reach Soviet territory, instead of the Pershing 2.

The Soviets threatened to leave the talks if deployment began in late 1983. President Reagan said the threat of deploying the missiles is necessary to indicate NATO's will. The missiles can be used as bargaining chips, he said, to be bargained away at the negotiating table for similar Soviet concessions.

Since their beginning in May 1982, the START talks have also made little headway. The United States has proposed ceilings for both countries of 5,000 warheads and 850 land- and sea-based missiles (leaving out bombers). The Russians counterproposed a ceiling of 1,800 missiles and bombers.

Likewise the MBFR talks have been stalled, waiting to see what happens with the other two.

None of the talks has taken a comprehensive approach to reducing arms and each would slow rather than stop the arms race. Freeze supporters say these are the flaws in Reagan's approach. An agreement to limit one type of missile is hard to achieve without considering the numbers of other missiles that remain. The Soviets are unlikely to agree to large reductions in their land-based missiles (which carry 71 percent of their warheads) without knowing whether the United States will reduce its submarine-based missiles (which carry 50 percent of our warheads).

Reagan also wished to link arms control progress to Soviet behavior in the rest of the world. To American eyes, the Soviets have adhered to the letter of peaceful coexistence but not to the spirit. They have not confronted the United States militarily but they have invaded Afghanistan, airlifted Cuban troops into Ethiopia, intervened in South Yemen, and supported the invasion of Cambodia by Vietnam. Hawks want to see an improvement in Soviet behavior in the rest of the world before agreeing to arms control. Linking these two factors together has further complicated the negotiations.

As arms-control talks stalled and the nuclear freeze movement gained momentum, the Reagan Administration curbed some of its bellicose talk. Reagan admitted that "Those who governed America throughout the nuclear age and we who govern it today have had to recognize that a nuclear war cannot be won and must never be fought." But he remained opposed to a nuclear freeze.

Both freeze and peace-through-strength supporters are concerned with avoiding nuclear war and maintaining national security. But they differ greatly in the ways they would achieve those ends. Some objections to the freeze have already been discussed: We can't trust the Russians to stick to a freeze. A freeze now would freeze the United States in a position of inferiority, some have said. The survival of democracy requires that we remain militarily superior to the Soviets. Other doubts arose as critics examined the freeze proposal closely:

(1) *A freeze is too simple.* It's fine as an expression of public concern but it's not a well-defined arms control proposal. The arms race is much too complex for the average American to understand and respond to intelligently.

"If you ask the average American what a Trident is, he thinks it's a stick of gum," said Representative Henry J. Hyde of Illinois. "If you ask him what the Minuteman is, he thinks it's an advertisement for an insurance company." Such a complex subject is best left to the experts, he concluded.

Freeze advocates have said that's what's wrong—arms control has been left to experts who don't always genuinely want the arms race to end. "We dare negotiate only from what the nuclear pundits call 'strength'—which serves as an excuse for not negotiating at all," commented George Ball, a former Under Secretary of State and Ambassador to the United Nations.

The treaties resulting from the talks are often so complicated the public gives up trying to understand and support them. The simplicity of the freeze is a political virtue; its benefits are so apparent the public will support it.

The comprehensiveness of the freeze gives it an advantage over the three separate arms talks in progress. The Soviets are more likely to agree to reduce their intermediate-range missiles if they know whether the United States will reduce their bombers and submarine-launched missiles. A freeze would be comprehensive and thus more likely to freeze general equality.

(2) *A freeze would freeze the arms race at too high a level.* The late Senator Henry Jackson said he was for a freeze but he wanted reductions first. He wanted to win Soviet agreement to deep cuts in nuclear arsenals, then freeze "at a sharply lower, safer, less menacing level of forces." He and Senator John Warner of Virginia pushed a resolution in Congress for reductions first, then a freeze.

When the freeze resolution passed the House in 1983, it had been amended to include reductions. The original intent of the freeze was to follow a freeze with negotiated reductions. The amendment imposed a "reasonable" time period for those reductions.

Freeze advocates have said seeking reductions first would just repeat previous failures. While negotiators chip away at the problems, both sides continue to build up their nuclear forces—indulging in a binge before the diet. SALT I took three years to be signed and ratified and SALT II six years to develop. As talks occur, technology overtakes the negotiations. New weapons are tested and developed before limits are agreed on for the old ones. New weapons are defended as "bargaining chips," but they are seldom bargained away. A freeze would first stop the escalation, then proceed with the diplomatic detail work.

(3) *Will the Russians go along with a freeze?* No one knows for sure, but past statements by their leaders indicate they would. Soviet President Leonid Brezhnev said in February 1982 that the Soviet Union was ready to agree to a halt in the production and stockpiling of nuclear weapons. But Brezhnev has since died, in November 1982.

The Russians have many reasons to welcome a freeze. Their domestic economy suffers from high inflation, agriculture failures that result in food shortages, low worker morale, and a shortage of consumer goods. The more money and resources they put into the military, the less is available for other needs.

If things are so bad, why do they keep pouring money into arms? They desperately want to keep up with the United States. George F. Kennan, a former ambassador to Moscow, sees their offensive efforts as motivated by defense. The Russians have been invaded three times by the West in this century, twice by Germany and by the western allies in 1919, including the United States. They lost twenty million people during World War II. As a result, they are determined that an invasion never will happen again. Anyone who dares attack Russia must know they will be destroyed in return.

The Soviet Union feels encircled by hostile powers— China, Iran, Pakistan, and Europe backed by the United States. They feel threatened by the large numbers of missiles aimed at them and they feel isolated, which reinforces an "us against them" mentality.

Kennan doubts the Russians are likely to invade Western Europe, because that would just increase their problems. They want to expand their influence in the world but not their responsibilities in another country. Since World War II their direct military intervention has taken place along their borders, for example. This extreme interpretation of their defense needs has made them a difficult neighbor, to say the least.

The United States has problems communicating with the Soviet Union. They seem secretive and closed, insecure, oversuspicious, and afraid of being tricked or outsmarted. Their penchant for propaganda sometimes has obscured their meaning. On the other hand they are not such monsters that they are just waiting for the right moment to launch a nuclear attack on us. They are as worried by our arsenals as we are by theirs.

The Soviet Union has an entrenched military-industrial complex, too, and their military leaders will be as reluctant as ours to give up new weapons. Thus the political will for peace must be strong on both sides. The growing fear of a nuclear holocaust may be the only sentiment strong enough to overcome the distrust between the two countries. We and the Russians, said Rev. Billy Graham, "have a common enemy, the possibility of nuclear war." A freeze will not resolve the ideological differences but it might prevent us from blowing up the world over our disagreements. Soviet President Yuri Andropov has also publicly stated that the Soviet Union will never *start* a nuclear war.

(4) *Does the freeze have a chance of being adopted, or is it just symbolic?* As the freeze resolution was debated in Congress, it was often described as "merely symbolic." Even if it passed both houses, the President would probably not implement it. The freeze campaign was an attempt to force Reagan to change his arms-control strategy and he remained unchanged.

Whether it is adopted or not, the freeze has aroused popular support for stopping the arms race. As the freeze grew as a political issue, national leaders responded. About seventy-five Representatives changed their No votes to Yes in the spring of 1983 on the freeze resolution. President Reagan stopped talking about winning nuclear war and undertook arms control negotiations.

Despite the shifts, Americans and their government are still not talking with a unified voice. Until there is more agreement on what United States nuclear policy should be, we will not be able to negotiate a freeze. Supporters believe the freeze could become policy, however, with a change of administration.

Until that happens, the freeze campaign has chosen the following legislative goals:

Passage of a freeze resolution by the Senate.

Stopping the new MIRVed ICBMs of the United States and the Soviet Union.

Achieving a one-year delay (from late 1983 to late 1984) in the deployment of new United States missiles in Europe in order to give the negotiators more time to reach an agreement. Such an agreement (from the INF talks) would include no new deployment of Euromissiles by either side and substantial reductions by the Soviets in the numbers of intermediate-range missiles they have already deployed.

The freeze campaign plans to speak out against all new United States and Soviet nuclear weapons, based on the belief that no additional weapons on either side can be justified. Opposing new weapons has always been difficult, because the weapons proponents include the Defense Department, three branches of the Armed Forces, and large defense contractors. The Pershing 2, for example, is a cherished project of the U.S. Army. A $19.3 million contract for development of the MX has been awarded to the Bechtel Corporation. Both the Secretary of Defense and the Secretary of State are former executive officers of the Bechtel Corporation. The three largest defense contractors—McDonnell Douglas, Lockheed, and General Dynamics—are all members of the American Security Council, an organization that supports the peace-through-strength position.

Another freeze-campaign plan is to work for a ban on the testing of nuclear weapons. Congress would be asked to legislate a moratorium effective by a certain date. The testing ban would continue as long as the Soviets also refrain from testing.

(5) *What are the alternatives to a freeze?* Discussion of the freeze has brought other ideas to the fore. One alternative is a nuclear build-down. A resolution in Congress sponsored by Senators William S. Cohen of Maine and

Sam Nunn of Georgia proposes that we seek a "mutual guaranteed, nuclear arms build-down." For every new warhead a superpower added, it would eliminate two older warheads. The sponsors hoped that less stabilizing warheads would be removed and more survivable, reliable weapons added. The Senators said such a build-down should appeal to both the freeze and modernization proponents because it would provide both reductions and modernization. Freeze supporters are concerned that the newest warheads are the most destabilizing because they are the most accurate.

Another alternative would be to shift from large, multiple warhead missiles capable of a first strike to smaller, less explosive, more numerous missiles. Such missiles would be more mobile and less vulnerable to a surprise attack but still capable of retaliation.

In the shift from forty-one Polaris submarines to twenty huge Trident submarines, for example, the number of hiding points for submarine-launched missiles is reduced. Each Trident has far more warheads than a Polaris, but they are centralized and more vulnerable if the Russians ever develop viable submarine detection systems.

The same is true of the MX; it's too big to hide and because of its accurate, multiple warheads it could be used as a first-strike weapon. The Commission on Strategic Forces (known as the Scowcroft Commission) suggested the United States consider building smaller ICBMs with single warheads that could be moved around in armored vehicles called Armadillos. This would sharply reduce the total number of warheads but make them less vulnerable to a preemptive attack. If the Russians could not be sure of destroying a large percentage of United States missiles in a first strike, the "window of vulnerability" would be closed.

(6) *If we freeze and reduce our nuclear weapons, how will we defend ourselves?* One response to this was given by Archbishop Raymond Hunthausen of Seattle: "I am struck by how much more terrified we Americans often are by talk of disarmament than by the march to nuclear war. We whose nuclear arms terrify millions around the globe are terrified by the thought of being without them."

Freeze supporters argue that we have so many nuclear weapons, we could eliminate most of them and still have enough for deterrence. A freeze would allow us to say enough is enough and return to MAD with a saner level of weaponry. Many people opposed to the continuation of the arms race are willing to tolerate some nuclear weapons—enough to use for retaliation if attacked.

How would the reductions occur? The freeze campaign has not spelled this out, but a former ambassador to Russia, George Kennan, proposes a 50 percent reduction in the stockpiles of each country within two years of a freeze, "without further wrangling among the experts," and then smaller steps to reduce the stockpiles further. The important thing is to begin the mutual reductions. Once started, both sides will gain trust in each other and the process.

Senator Albert Gore of Tennessee has suggested a plan whereby the most dangerous nuclear weapons should be eliminated first, namely the first-strike weapons that can attack with little warning. These would be the MX, Trident II, Minuteman III, and the Soviet SS-17, 18, and 19—the land-based MIRVed missiles. As reductions occurred, each side would become more sure the other could not pull off a successful surprise attack.

Disarmament advocates who are not spokespeople for the freeze have suggested some other alternatives. One way to reduce our dependence on nuclear weapons would be to strengthen our conventional forces. Western countries have been relying on technology rather than large armies for defense. But using nuclear weapons to defend Europe risks obliterating it in the process. Many Europeans are more worried about the prospect of nuclear war than they are about the Russians. Preparing to defend Europe from an invasion without nuclear arms would eliminate the need for a first-use policy.

A large increase in conventional forces would cost more than nuclear weapons and might provoke resistance to the draft. Some improvements could be made, however, without an increase: better antitank defenses, the use of inexpensive precision-guided munitions such as antitank guided missiles, prepositioning of supplies, and new systems for moving forces to the battlefields. After such improvements the large number of tactical weapons deployed in Europe could be reduced.

Another plan would shift totally away from missiles deployed within the land space of a nation. The Campaign for Nuclear Disarmament wants Britain to adopt a nonnuclear defense policy. All nuclear weapons would be removed from British soil and only a retaliatory force on submarines retained.

A freeze between the United States and the Soviet Union would enhance world security by giving other countries an incentive to curb the development and spread of nuclear weapons. As part of the Nonproliferation Treaty, both countries and the United Kingdom agreed to "pursue negotiations . . . relating to cessation of the nuclear arms race at an early date. . . ." The snail's pace of those negotiations has not made it realistic to ask other countries to renounce their own nuclear weapons in the meantime.

Freeze advocates maintain that a freeze will actually enhance our security, by eliminating first-strike weapons and the hair-trigger state of readiness that accompanies them. It would allow us to use our resources to meeting other needs, to developing domestic energy sources, for example, so we would not feel obliged to defend Middle Eastern oil supplies.

Despite all the weapons built in the last decade, Americans feel less secure from nuclear war now than ten years ago. The prevention of nuclear war is no longer a technical problem; it is a political problem whose solution must be found through international political means.

THE GROUND ZERO CENTER
FOR NONVIOLENT ACTION

The living room of a small farmhouse is crowded with about twenty-five people seated on old sofas, chairs, and the floor, talking quietly. Headlights tell of the arrival of others as cars pull into the dirt and gravel driveway. The farmhouse is on a quiet, rural, wooded peninsula on Puget Sound in Washington state. Its backyard extends to the fence of the giant submarine base where Trident submarines are refueled and fitted with nuclear bombs.

The gathering is the Wednesday-night community meeting of the Ground Zero Center for Nonviolent Action, a group of people who for eight years have been protesting each stage of the base's development. When the U.S.S. *Ohio*, the first of the Tridents, arrived in August 1982 to be fitted, it was "greeted" by 7,000 demonstrators on land and a 21-boat Peace Flotilla.

This evening the focus is on land transportation of nuclear weapons. The second Trident, the U.S.S. *Michigan*, had arrived at the base that morning but the center had decided not to organize a protest. After describing their individual feelings, actions, and reactions to the arrival of the *Michigan*, the group turns to hear from a young couple seated at the far end of the room. They are two United Methodist ministers who have been organizing peace activities in the rural communities they serve.

The couple—Paul Jeffrey and Lyda Pierce—live in Elma, Washington, three blocks from the railroad tracks that pass through town. When they were first assigned to three churches in the area, Paul acquired the habit of taking long walks with their beagle, Bishop. Those walks took him along the tracks and through the railyards. It was there, one day, he discovered containers marked Explosive A. Friends had told Paul and Lyda that missile motors are transported from Salt Lake City, Utah, to the Trident base at Bangor, Washington. (Missile motors are the solid stage that fuels the Trident missiles.) Since that discovery, the arms race has seemed much closer to home. Paul and Lyda have led their community in monitoring and "vigiling": learning to recognize and report when nuclear weapons are being shipped on the tracks and holding vigils on an overpass when such trains pass through. They talk about ripping down the shroud of invisibility that keeps people from noticing what moves through their towns.

The ministers are part of the Agape Community, a group of people in thirty-five towns and cities along the tracks who watch for nuclear shipments to the Trident base. One week after this meeting the Agape Community will hold peace vigils as a white train believed to be carrying hydrogen bombs travels through five states from the Pantex plant outside Amarillo, Texas, to Bangor.

"We decided that wherever the train goes, we're going . . . to provide a nonviolent protest," said Jim Douglass, a founder of the center. "We want as many people as possible to see this train."

The Agape Community was formed at the farmhouse in the nonviolent tradition the Ground Zero Center practices. It is a tradition based on the work and teachings of Mahatma Gandhi and Martin Luther King, Jr. In addition to Protestant ministers, Catholic sisters and Buddhist monks volunteer at the center. The monks and local volunteers are building a Peace Pagoda on part of the 3.8 acres (1.44 ha) of land the center owns. It will be the first such pagoda in North America.

The freeze is not a central issue for the center. They have concentrated instead on taking nonviolent action in their local community. At a demonstration of 4,000 people at the base in May 1978, hundreds were arrested and 176 were convicted of trespassing for "going over the fence"—climbing over the fence around the Trident base. Since then, the center has shifted from large demonstrations to communicating with the community. "We want to be good neighbors rather than outside protesters," said Douglass, "and there's an ongoing task of education and deepening our own sense of responsibility."

On Thursday mornings, volunteers give leaflets to workers who drive through the Trident gates early in the morning and they encourage military people to come to their community meetings. Several Trident workers have resigned from their jobs at the base to avoid working on nuclear weapons. Derald Thompson, for example, left a job training crew members for the Trident submarine. He now works for a firm in California.

Some of the volunteers have committed themselves to civil disobedience. "If we refuse to cooperate with the government's building nuclear weapons, we can do it," said Jeanne Clark, a member of the Dominican Order. "I believe it is important to be an obstacle in the deployment of first-strike weapons."

Groups like the Ground Zero Center have dug in for the long run in the peace movement. They have decided to work in their own backyards to change people's minds. Such groups will continue to work for peace whether the freeze succeeds or fades.

7

BEYOND
A FREEZE

"In a democracy we are all responsible for pushing the button," goes a popular saying of the nuclear weapons freeze campaign. Actually there is no button; two keys must be turned simultaneously by two people to fire the missiles. Whatever the mechanism, the implication is clear. If nuclear war happens, we are all responsible because we didn't act to prevent it.

What do you think about the use of nuclear weapons? Under what circumstances, if any, would you be willing to "push the button"? Consider the following situation.*
You are President and you have just been told the computers indicate that nuclear missiles are about to attack all areas of the United States. This attack does not come completely out of the blue. A full-scale war between Iran and Iraq has spread throughout the Middle East. Both the United States and the Soviet Union have been moving ships and troops toward the area to protect oil supplies. You know that the computer warning could be a false alarm—there have been many—and that a nuclear exchange will probably destroy both countries. You also

*paraphrased from *Decision Making in the Nuclear Age*, a curriculum from Educators for Social Responsibility.

know that if you don't counterattack now, you lose the best chance for an effective retaliation. You have three minutes to decide what to do. Do you hope it's a mistake and do nothing or order the keys turned?

Bringing this dilemma to your attention is one of the purposes of the freeze movement. Another is to point toward a solution. The preceding chapters have presented the freeze as one way to prevent such a predicament. Other viewpoints on preventing nuclear war have also been presented. This last chapter will discuss what is likely to happen in the second half of the 1980s, then suggest what one person can do to help prevent nuclear war.

The freeze campaign has mustered popular support for arms control. The names gathered on petitions will keep the freeze issue alive through the 1984 elections. Beyond 1984, enthusiasm for a freeze may fade or increase as long, complex arms control negotiations continue without immediate success. The concern about preventing nuclear war, however, will not go away. "The world's other problems become meaningless if we don't solve this one and do it quickly," said Father Theodore Hesburgh, President of the University of Notre Dame.

If a freeze is adopted, some of the following steps are likely:

(1) *A treaty spelling out the terms of the freeze, what is included, and how it will be verified.*

(2) *Negotiated reductions, especially in destabilizing (first-strike) weapons.*

(3) *Conversion of nuclear arms industries to other purposes.* The government may provide some aid to industries and workers affected by a freeze. Factories, scientists, engineers, computer programmers, and submarine repair people could be put to work building mass transit systems, developing new energy sources, or producing planes. Many local groups, such as the Puget Sound Conversion Project, the Bendix Conversion Project in Kansas

City, and the Pinellas Conversion Project in St. Petersburg, Florida, are already planning such changes.

(4) *Stopping the spread of nuclear weapons.* Once the superpowers agree to halt their own production of nuclear weapons, they will be in a better position to ask other countries to stop. Unless such production is stopped, 40 countries will be able to make a nuclear bomb by 1990. The 123 countries that signed the 1968 Nonproliferation Treaty have already agreed not to produce a bomb. But many countries that could build a bomb did not sign, including Israel, South Africa, Pakistan, Algeria, India, Egypt, and Iraq. Any country with a nuclear reactor can convert the byproducts to build a bomb. As more nuclear weapons are produced, the chances increase they might be used by terrorists, an insane dictator, or just passionate enemies.

(5) *The creation of nuclear free zones.* Several areas of the world are nuclear free: Antarctica, outer space, and Latin America. The Latin American Nuclear Free Zone was proclaimed in 1968. All the Latin American nations except Cuba agreed they will use nuclear materials and facilities only for peaceful purposes.

Similar efforts have been made to declare the Indian Ocean a Zone of Peace and to create a Nuclear Free Pacific, including the Pacific Ocean islands where missiles are tested. Countries like Sweden and Norway have labeled themselves nuclear free. The END campaign in Europe has the goal of removing all nuclear weapons from European soil, country by country. One hundred and sixty towns in Belgium have declared themselves "denuclearized," as have some neighborhoods in the United States. A grass-roots campaign originating in New Zealand urges people to declare their own homes and workplaces Nuclear Weapon Free zones.

(6) *Elimination of nuclear weapons.* The spread of nuclear free zones could lead eventually to the total elimination of nuclear weapons. If all nuclear weapons in the United States and the Soviet Union were retired when they became obsolete, for example, by the year 2020 the strategic nuclear forces of both countries would be virtually eliminated. The sooner we get rid of them all, some people say, the safer we will be.

Others say the total elimination of nuclear weapons is naive and impossible. "There is no way to regain nuclear virginity," said Vice Admiral John Marshall Lee. The knowledge of how to make bombs will remain even if the weapons are removed. Security will come from controlling nuclear weapons rather than eliminating them.

If a freeze is not adopted, efforts to curb the arms race could proceed in several ways:

(1) *Continued arms control negotiations.* The talks begun during the Reagan Administration may continue, with the immediate goal of reducing the number of intermediate-range missiles in Europe.

Broader, more all-inclusive talks, such as SALT III, could outline a gradual end to nuclear arms production and a reduction by both sides equally of their stockpiles. Such talks lack the immediacy of a freeze but would continue the long negotiating process the United States and the Soviet Union have been involved in almost continuously since 1969 when SALT I began.

A halt to the testing of nuclear weapons is another possibility. Former SALT negotiator Paul Warnke formed a Committee for National Security to revive public interest in a Comprehensive Test Ban Treaty. Such a treaty would prohibit underground tests, as well as the atmospheric, outer space, underwater, and underground testing above a certain threshold that are already prohibited by treaties. Negotiations for such a ban began between the United States, the Soviet Union, and the United Kingdom in 1977, but the Reagan Administration postponed them indefinitely in 1980 so new weapons could be developed.

One obstacle to such a treaty has been verification. A breakthrough occurred, however, when the three countries agreed in 1978 they would allow seismic monitoring stations to be constructed on their territory. The stations would listen for the waves produced by the testing of nuclear devices. With this groundwork accomplished, Warnke would like to see negotiations begin again.

(2) *Unilateral peace initiatives.* Freeze advocates emphasize that a freeze must be mutual—undertaken by both countries at the same time. Some peace groups, like the American Friends Service Committee and the World without War Council, have urged the United States to take a unilateral action (by itself) in the expectation the Soviet Union would respond in kind. Having begun the arms race, we could suggest the way out.

In 1977, for example, more than 12,000 scientists, engineers, and other professionals of the Union of Concerned Scientists recommended to the President that the United States adopt a moratorium on testing and challenge the Soviet Union to do the same. Or the Soviet Union could take a unilateral step like stopping further development of one of its new strategic weapons and wait for a similar response from the United States.

Unilateral initiatives have not won popular backing in the United States because of the deep distrust of the Russians. But they have worked in the past. In 1963 President Kennedy announced the United States would not test any nuclear weapons in the atmosphere. Russia soon followed suit, and the Partial Test Ban Treaty was signed two months later.

(3) *A No First Use of nuclear weapons policy.* The United States could announce that we would never be the first to use nuclear weapons. The Russians have already said this, but the United States has not because NATO reserves the right to use nuclear weapons first if Europe is overwhelmed by a conventional attack.

Adopting a No First Use policy might necessitate building up U.S. conventional forces as part of NATO's defense. But the distinction between conventional and nuclear warfare could more easily be maintained if war started.

If a freeze or other attempts succeed in controlling the arms race in the next few years, attention can turn to peacemaking. What must happen in the long run to preserve this planet?

Somehow we must "get along" with the Russians—not agree with them, or defer to them, or intimidate them, but realize it is in the self-interest of both countries to prevent nuclear war.

"The time has come for the two superpowers to recognize the United States is not the enemy. The Soviet Union is not the enemy. Nuclear weapons are the enemy of both nations and of all mankind," said a retired admiral. Because each country could easily destroy the other, we are dependent on one another's good will.

Actions to demonstrate that good will have already been made. The Presbyterian Church of the United States sent forty representatives to Russia in the spring of 1983. Thirty Seattle residents carried a letter with 44,000 signatures to Tashkent in the Soviet Union. The letter calls on citizens of both countries to work together for peaceful solutions to conflicts and to prevent nuclear war.

A People to People Peace Pledge was initiated in 1983 to establish five million individual contacts between the American and Russian people by July 4, 1984. People who sign, pledge to each other never to participate in an invasion or occupation of the other's homeland or to approve the shelling, bombing, or use of nuclear missiles against the other's country (unless in retaliation).

Such efforts to make peace on a people-to-people basis have been matched by campaigns through national and international institutions. Legislation has been introduced in the U.S. Congress to establish a National Peace Academy, to teach peacemaking skills. The Women's

International League for Peace and Freedom's STAR campaign (Stop the Arms Race) collected signatures to bring to the United Nations Special Session on Disarmament. An international freeze petition is being circulated in forty countries.

One symbolic event, in 1985, will be the tying of a ribbon around the Pentagon on the fortieth anniversary of the bombing of Hiroshima and Nagasaki. In contrast to the bombing, the ribbon is to be lovingly created—sewn, embroidered, woven, hooked, or quilted—"to remind our nation that we love the earth and its people."

A shift in our way of thinking has begun. Since war is likely to destroy the whole planet, it has lost its usefulness as a means of solving disagreements. The fact of our shared humanity, says writer Jonathan Schell in *The Fate of the Earth*, must demand more allegiance than national sovereignty. Such a change in thinking comes slowly, however; perhaps too slowly.

On a day when the principal calls and asks for help at the school barbecue, he also mentions his concern about a trainload of nuclear warheads passing through the state, about a hundred miles (160 km) from the school. It's not far enough. Parents and educators worry about what good all their fine schools will do if their children die in a nuclear war.

Worrying is recognizing there's a problem. Moving beyond worrying requires a feeling that it is possible to do something to prevent nuclear war. Caldicott, Lipton, Mattes, Vaughan, and others involved in the peace movement talk about *empowerment*—the feeling of power that comes when people begin to do something together.

"In the face of catastrophe to do nothing and be passive is very depressing because you feel so powerless," writes Helen Caldicott. "But if you *try* and do something, it's the most exciting action you can take. . . . I say to myself 'Even if the bombs go off, at least I'll be able to say I tried.' "

Merely signing a name on a freeze petition is a big step for some. Others, who have been activists for peace for a long time, are refusing to cooperate with the building of nuclear weapons. This refusal takes several forms. One is withholding the taxes that would go for nuclear weapons. Another is "going over the fence" at Vandenburg Air Force Base to protest the testing of new missiles. Two young men scaled the fence of a Minuteman silo near Great Falls, Montana, planted wheat seeds, laid a cross on the silo cover, and sat down to eat bread while awaiting the security officers.

In Britain 15,000 to 30,000 demonstrators, mostly women, have twice formed a human "chain of peace" around the Greenham Common Air Force Base where 96 U.S. cruise missiles will be deployed. They linked hands and stood shoulder to shoulder around its 9-mile (14.48-km) perimeter and lit candles as darkness fell.

A similar Women's Peace Encampment was held near the Seneca Army Depot in Rochester, New York in the summer of 1983. The 11,000-acre (4452 ha) base is probably a storage site for neutron bombs and possibly for Pershing 2 missile warheads. The depot is the main point on the East Coast from which nuclear weapons are shipped to Europe. Forty-some women camped outside Boeing's cruise missile production site near Kent, Washington.

Refusing to ignore is a necessary step toward refusing to cooperate. Methodist ministers hold peace vigils along railroad tracks when nuclear weapons are being shipped, so people can't ignore what's coming down the tracks. A 1,000-member citizens organization in Wisconsin and Michigan wants the rest of the country to know the Navy is planning to install a "doomsday trigger" in the northern woods there. Project ELF would install a large radio transmitter that will send one-way messages to nuclear submarines, conceivably to coordinate an attack.

**Peace demonstrators marched to the
Boeing Company's cruise missile production
site near Kent, Washington, where they
participated in a nuclear arms protest encampment.**

Much of the active resistance to nuclear weapons is religiously based. Many Quakers have long been pacifists, but they have been joined by other religious groups with varying degrees of pacifism. The Sojourners, an evangelical Christian fellowship in Washington, D. C., issued a "new abolitionist covenant," which calls for believers to work for disarmament. "We will offer faith in God as an alternative to trust in the bomb," the covenant reads.

The bishops pastoral letter asked Catholics to pray and fast for peace by returning to meatless Fridays. "We seek to encourage a public attitude which sets stringent limits on the kind of actions our Government will take on nuclear policy in our names," it said.

Some individual bishops have led more active resistance. Bishop Leroy T. Matthiesen in Amarillo, Texas, urged his parishioners to stop working at the Pantex plant there, which assembles nuclear bombs. Archbishop Raymond G. Hunthausen of Seattle has decided to withhold half of his federal income taxes in protest against the arms race. "We must take special responsibility for what is in our own backyard," he said, in this case the Trident submarine base on Puget Sound.

Much of the most active protest centers around military bases with a role in nuclear weapons—the Trident submarine base at Bangor, Washington, where submarines refuel and are fitted with nuclear weapons; Vandenburg Air Force Base in California, a missile test site; the General Dynamics Electric Boat Division in Groton, Connecticut, where the Trident submarines are built; Lockheed Missiles and Space Company, in Sunnyvale, California, which makes Trident missiles; King's Bay, Georgia, the proposed site for the Atlantic Trident base; and the Rocky Flats Plant near Colorado Springs, Colorado, where the triggers for nuclear warheads are manufactured. Nuclear weapons are now stored or deployed in thirty-four states and three U.S. territories. Although most people are reluctant to engage in illegal

Several hundred people marched to the General Dynamics Electric Boat Division, in Groton, Connecticut, in June of 1983 to protest the commissioning of the Trident submarine U.S.S. *Florida*.

actions like trespassing on a military base or sailing into the path of a nuclear submarine, such activism may increase if the arms race is not curbed.

WHAT YOU CAN DO

Preventing nuclear war is a tall order. We got ourselves into this situation, however, and we can get ourselves out. People like Lipton and Mattes reorganized their working lives; Paul Jolly devoted a summer that changed his life; others go to meetings or write letters.

Young people have also been involved in the peace movement. The Children's Campaign for Nuclear Disarmament, which began as six children working together in Plainfield, Vermont, took 5,000 letters to Washington in 1982. The Campaign now has 75 chapters. The Student/ Teacher Organization to Prevent Nuclear War (STOP) publishes a newsletter for high school students.

If you want to do something, here are some actions to consider:

1. Read, educate yourself. Learn all about nuclear issues. It's not top secret or something that only experts can understand. Retired Admiral Gene R. LaRocque recalled, "When I was in the Pentagon we used to foster this notion that we military men had a special knowledge about how to defend our nation, information not available to other citizens." But on the subject of avoiding war, the Admiral said, "You have as much to say as the highest ranking general or admiral."

2. Talk to other people about the threat of nuclear war. Listen to what they have to say. Talk to someone with a different point of view from your own; find out what you agree on.

3. Vote, when you are 18. If all the 18-to-35-year-olds who usually don't vote did, politics would change. Democracy is powerful if you use it.

4. Write letters: to newspaper editors, public officials, radio and television stations, relatives, and friends. Write a letter a week for peace. Ask your congressional representative how she or he intends to vote on the freeze and new weapons programs.

5. Join an organization that suits your views and interests. Most national groups have local chapters. Consult the list at the end of this book.

6. "Don't agonize—organize." Organize other people or an event, a letter-writing campaign, a school assembly on nuclear issues, a debate. Hold a meeting, show a film. Films on nuclear issues are available from libraries and national organizations.

7. Try to place the Earthrise picture (or other views of the earth from space) in your school, church, or public buildings.

8. Ask for global education in your school.

9. Think about the fantasies you are playing out in nuclear war video games.

10. Raise money to offer for the dismantling of one nuclear warhead.

11. Gather signatures on a petition to support arms control.

12. Buy a ticket for a rock concert supporting peace.

13. Wear a T-shirt for peace.

14. Make a nuclear map, showing the effect of a nuclear bomb on your city or town (see the bibliography for a source of information).

15. Live your own life in a peaceful manner; resolve conflicts without violence.

16. Celebrate life.

A general turned statesman, President Eisenhower, once said, "People in the long run are going to do more to promote peace than are governments. I think that people want peace so much that one of these days governments had better get out of their way and let them have it."

ORGANIZATIONS AND SOURCES OF INFORMATION

Many groups are part of the freeze and peace movements. Some have local chapters you can join. Check the phonebook in your town or city or write to the national organization to find out if there is a local chapter in your area.

Other national organizations are good sources of information. They will send you brochures, pamphlets, fact sheets, article reprints, and bibliographies, for the cost of mailing or a small fee.

The main freeze organization is:

Nuclear Weapons Freeze Campaign
National Clearinghouse
4144 Lindell Blvd., Suite 404
St. Louis, MO 63108

The national clearinghouse will send a Freeze Campaign Information Packet, including fact sheets, for $3.00 prepaid. The quarterly Freeze newsletter is $10 a year. The freeze campaign has chapters in all fifty states and almost all congressional districts.

An organization of particular interest to students is:

STOP
Student/Teacher Organization to Prevent Nuclear War
Box 232
Northfield, MA 01360

STOP is a new national organization for high school teachers and students. It has local chapters in high schools and a newsletter for and by high school students. The organization is "committed to informing . . . local school communities of the dangers of the nuclear arms race, and the actions young people can take to reduce these dangers."

Other organizations are as follows:

American Friends Service Committee
1501 Cherry St.
Philadelphia, PA 19102

Thirty-five Peace Education Offices around the country. National Action/Research on the Military Industrial Complex (NARMIC) will send a list of publications and resources (same address).

The Center for Defense Information
600 Maryland Ave. SW
Washington, DC 20024

A ten-year-old organization of retired military officers who educate Congress and the executive branch on facts about military spending. *Defense Monitor* published ten times a year. Send $1 for *Nuclear War Prevention Kit,* telling how individuals can make their voices heard.

Children's Campaign for Nuclear Disarmament
14 Everit St.
New Haven, CT 06511

Clergy and Laity Concerned (CALC)
198 Broadway
New York, NY 10038

40 local offices. *CALC Reports* are available.

Council for a Livable World
11 Beacon St.
Boston, MA 02108

Nuclear Arms Control Hotline: (202) 543-0006.

Educators for Social Responsibility
639 Massachusetts Ave.
Cambridge, MA 02139

This organization has developed a curriculum called "Decision-making in the Nuclear Age." Local branches. Bibliography available.

Federation of American Scientists
307 Massachusetts Ave. NE
Washington, DC 20002

Newsletter *Countdown.*

Ground Zero
806 Fifteenth St. NW, Suite 421
Washington, DC 20005

Local branches. Materials order form. (See Bibliography.)

Nuclear Information and Resource Center
1346 Connecticut Ave. NW, Fourth floor
Washington, DC 20036

Brochures describe teacher's resource guides and kits on nuclear weapons and nuclear power issues. *Groundswell,* monthly journal.

Physicians for Social Responsibility
639 Massachusetts Ave.
Cambridge, MA 02139

Local branches.

Promoting Enduring Peace
P.O. Box 103
Woodmont, CT 06460

Reprints of articles on nuclear weapons issues.

SANE (Citizen's Organization for a SANE World)
711 G St., SE
Washington, DC 20003

Pamphlet, *Deadly Standoff: The U.S.–Soviet Military Balance.*

Union of Concerned Scientists
26 Church St.
Cambridge, MA 02238

Pamphlet, *The Arms Control Debate*

United Campuses to Prevent Nuclear War
1346 Connecticut Ave. NW
Washington, DC 20036

United States Arms Control and Disarmament Agency
320 21st St. NW
Washington, DC 20451

Women's International League for Peace and Freedom
1213 Race St.
Philadelphia, PA 19107

World Peacemakers
2025 Massachusetts Ave.
Washington, DC 20036

For information on the peace-through-strength view, contact:

American Security Council
The Coalition for Peace Through Strength
Boston, VA 22713

Booklet, *How Realistic Is the Nuclear Freeze Proposal?* $2.00. *Washington Report*, newsletter.

GLOSSARY OF NUCLEAR WEAPONS TERMS

ABM: Antiballistic missile designed to destroy attacking missiles. The United States and the Soviet Union are each limited to one ABM site with no more than 100 antiballistic missiles under the 1974 ABM Treaty.

ALCM: Air-launched cruise missile. An ALCM can be launched from bombers—such as B-52s or B-1Bs—and will be stationed at U.S. Air Force bases.

Ballistic missile: A missile that travels in a trajectory, without wing or power, once it is guided during takeoff.

Bilateral: Describes an action taken by both sides and affecting both sides.

B-1B: A new strategic bomber to replace the B-52.

B-52: The main strategic bomber of the U.S. Air Force, capable of carrying nuclear weapons thousands of miles.

Conventional: Nonnuclear military forces, including land, sea, and air weapons and manpower.

Counterforce: Having the accuracy and explosive power to destroy enemy military forces, especially ICBMs in their silos.

Countervalue: Having the ability to destroy population targets like cities; need not be as accurate.

Cruise missile: A small, pilotless guided missile, which flies at very low altitudes to avoid radar detection. A cruise missile is 20 feet (6 m) long, looks like a torpedo, ranges up to 1,500 miles (2414 km), and can carry nuclear warheads that deliver up to 200 kilotons.

Deploy: To put soldiers, materials, or weapons in a place where they are ready to use.

Destabilizing weapon: A weapon whose accuracy and speed decreases the amount of time the opponent has to react to it. The Pershing 2 is considered a destabilizing weapon, as is the MX.

Firebreak: The threshold between the use of conventional and nuclear weapons, like a break created in a forest to prevent the spread of fire.

Fission: The process of splitting the nucleus of an atom, which releases energy.

First-strike weapon: A weapon that because of its accuracy and speed could be used first in a surprise attack.

Freeze: To call a halt to the testing, development, or deployment of nuclear weapons.

Fusion: A thermonuclear reaction in which the nuclei of lighter atoms join to form the nuclei of heavier atoms, releasing energy in the process. Fusion releases more energy than fission. The hydrogen bomb is a fusion bomb; the atom bomb is a fission bomb.

GLCM: A ground-launched cruise missile, which is mobile and is launched from a launcher.

Ground Zero: The point on the earth directly below the center of a nuclear explosion.

ICBM: Intercontinental ballistic missile. ICBMs are land-based and can carry warheads from one continent to another, flying above the earth's atmosphere, reaching its target in about 30 minutes.

Kiloton: Explosive power equivalent to 1,000 tons of TNT.

Laser weapons: Weapons that use intense beams of light to destroy targets.

Launcher: A means of launching a missile, for example, a

five-ton truck that can lift a missile into an upright position and fire it.

Launch-on-warning: A computerized warning system that would fire nuclear weapons automatically when surveillance satellites signal a possible enemy attack.

Limited war: A war using some nuclear weapons, such as tactical nuclear weapons, that would not escalate into an all-out nuclear exchange.

MAD: Mutual Assured Destruction. A situation in which each side knows the other side could destroy it.

MARV: Maneuverable reentry vehicle. MARVed missiles have warheads whose course can be changed while the missile is in the air.

Medium-range missiles: Missiles capable of flying hundreds of miles rather than thousands of miles. The Soviet SS-20 and the American Pershing 2 are medium- (or intermediate-) range missiles.

Megaton: Explosive power equivalent to 1,000,000 tons of TNT.

Minuteman: A U.S. land-based ICBM. The Minuteman II has one warhead. The Minuteman III has three MIRVs (warheads). Some Minuteman IIIs have the newer MK-12A warheads with greater explosive power and accuracy.

MIRV: Multiple Independently Targetable Reentry Vehicle. A MIRVed missile carries from two to twelve warheads, each of which can be directed at a different target.

MX: Missile Experimental. A new U.S. ICBM which would be equipped with ten MIRVs.

Nonproliferation: Stopping the further development and spread of nuclear weapons.

Nuclear-free zone: Area in which nuclear weapons would not be produced, stored, deployed, or used.

Nuclear warfighting capabilities: The ability to carry on a protracted nuclear war.

Neutron bomb: A nuclear bomb that releases neutrons which kill people but produce little blast or contamination. The area and buildings remain relatively intact and can be reoccupied shortly thereafter.

Silo: A hardened (with concrete and steel) container in the ground. It contains a ballistic missile and the equipment for firing it.

SLBM: A submarine-launched ballistic missile.

SLCM: A sea-launched cruise missile, can be fired from warships and attack submarines.

Strategic weapons: Long-range weapons capable of reaching the United States from the Soviet Union, for example, and vice versa.

Tactical weapons: Short-range weapons, intended for use within one region or battlefield.

Triad: Three-pronged nuclear defense: ground-launched missiles, submarines, and bombers.

Unilateral: Describes an action taken by one side, such as a unilateral initiative in which one nation would take an independent action to signal its willingness to negotiate disarmament agreements with another nation or nations.

Verification: The means by which abiding by an arms control treaty is checked.

Warhead: The part of a missile that contains the explosive.

Window of vulnerability: A window in time, used by President Ronald Reagan to describe a period during which U.S. ICBMs would be vulnerable to a Soviet surprise attack.

BIBLIOGRAPHY

BOOKS

Barash, David P., and Lipton, Judith E. *Stop Nuclear War! A Handbook.* New York: Grove Press, 1982.

Caldicott, Helen. *Nuclear Madness: What You Can Do.* New York: Bantam Books, 1981.

Cox, Arthur M. *Russian Roulette: The Superpower Game.* New York: New York Times Books, 1982.

Ford, Daniel; Kendall, Henry; and Nadis, Steven. *Beyond the Freeze: Steps to Avoid Nuclear War.* Boston: Beacon Press, 1982.

Gottlieb, Sanford. *What About the Russians?* Northfield, MA: Student/Teacher Organization to Prevent Nuclear War, 1982.

Ground Zero. *Nuclear War, What's in It for You?* New York: Pocket Books, 1982.

Ground Zero. *What About the Russians—and Nuclear War?* New York: Pocket Books, 1983.

Hatfield, Mark O., and Kennedy, Edward M. *Freeze! How You Can Help Prevent Nuclear War.* New York: Bantam Books, 1982.

Mattes, Kitty C. *In Your Hands, A Citizen's Guide to the Arms Race.* 140 West State Street, Ithaca, New York 14850: Kitty C. Mattes, 1981.

Scheer, Robert. *With Enough Shovels: Reagan, Bush, and Nuclear War.* New York: Random House, 1982.

Schell, Jonathan. *The Fate of the Earth.* New York: Knopf, 1982.

Taylor, L.B. *The Nuclear Arms Race.* New York: Franklin Watts, 1982.

BOOKLETS, PAMPHLETS, ARTICLES

Cartoonists Against the Arms Race. *A Cartoon History of the Nuclear Arms Race.* Cartoonists Against the Arms Race Publications, 1982.
Available from: The Church Council of Greater Seattle or Zephyr Graphics, Suite 240, 507 Third Ave., Seattle, WA 98104.

Center for Defense Information. *Nuclear War Prevention Kit.*
Available from: Center for Defense Information, 303 Capitol Gallery West, 600 Maryland Ave. SW, Washington, DC 20024.

Forsberg, Randall. "A Bilateral Nuclear Weapons Freeze." *Scientific American* 247 (November 1982): 52–61. #744, Scientific-American Offprints.
Available from: W. H. Freeman & Co., 660 Market St., San Francisco, CA 94104.

———. "Call to Halt the Nuclear Arms Race."
Available from: Nuclear Weapons Freeze Campaign, National Clearinghouse, 4144 Lindell Blvd., St. Louis, MO 63108.

———. "Is a U.S.–Soviet Nuclear Weapons Freeze Possible?" *CALC Report* 393 (October 1980).
Available from: Clergy and Laity Concerned, 198 Broadway, New York, N.Y. 10038.

Hatfield, Mark O. "The Age of Anxiety: Emerging Nuclear Tensions in the 1980s." *Hatfield Backgrounder* 193 (June 1981).
Available from: Senator Mark O. Hatfield, Washington, DC 20510.
Norwich Peace Center. *Freeze It! A Citizen's Guide to Reversing the Nuclear Arms Race.* 1982.
Available from: Norwich Peace Center, Box 283, Norwich, VT 05055
Nuclear Mapping Kit. Tips for making a map of the effect of a nuclear bomb on your city or town.
Available from: New Manhattan Project, 15 Rutherford Place, New York, N.Y. 10003.
Union of Concerned Scientists. *The Arms Control Debate.*
Available from: UCS, 26 Church St., Cambridge, MA 02138.
Union of Concerned Scientists. *A Framework for a New National Security Policy.*

FILMS

Countdown for America. The American Security Council Foundation.
If You Love This Planet. National Film Board of Canada.
No First Use. Union of Concerned Scientists.
War Without Winners. Center for Defense Information.
Available from: Center for Defense Information, 303 Capitol Gallery West, 600 Maryland Ave. SW, Washington, DC 20024.

INDEX